MONEY *IS* EVERYTHING

MONEY
IS PERSONAL FINANCE
FOR THE BRAVE NEW ECONOMY
EVERYTHING

AMANDA REAUME

With a Foreword by Dan Acland

TYCHO
PRESS

CONTENTS

PART TWO SPENDING IT

PART FOUR SAVING IT

13 DISPOSABLE INCOME 191

Do You Want to Be a Millionaire or Just Live Like One? •
Allocating Your Disposable Income

FROM THE SOURCE: WHAT SHOULD I DO WITH MY DISPOSABLE INCOME?

14 SAVING VS. PAYING OFF DEBT 199

You Can't Do Everything • Ways to Use Money, Ranked

FROM THE SOURCE: CHOOSING BETWEEN SAVING AND PAYING OFF DEBT

15 INVESTING 207

Ways to Pump Up Your Money • Uncommon Investment Options •
Not All Stocks Are Created Equal • Have More Than One Basket •
100K By 30: Why Starting Early Is Important

FROM THE SOURCE: WHY SHOULD I INVEST?

HACKS 220

FOREWORD

BY DAN ACLAND

MILLENNIALS Optimistic, entrepreneurial, connected, team-oriented, and highly adept at multitasking. If you were born between 1980 and 1999, that's what researchers say you are. But also overconfident to a fault, and thus prone to discouragement when confronted with life's setbacks. Setbacks that you are all the more likely to have encountered because you came of age during the Great Recession. And while your generation, the "Millennial Generation," is the most educated in American history, many of you are entering the working world with mountains of student debt, and little in the way of good credit.

Meanwhile, the world you have inherited is one in which personal initiative and personal responsibility have become indispensable. Gone are the days when education guaranteed you a first job, and that job led to another, and so on until retirement. In today's fragmented labor market, you must become your own brand and sell yourself like the hottest of new, new things. And you will have to do so again and again, because in today's economy you will have, on average, 25 jobs over the course of your career. Gone too are the days when large institutions—employers, unions, and the state—shielded you from life's biggest risks. Now each individual is expected to provide their own safety net, with wisely invested retirement savings, health insurance (which you are increasingly likely to have to provide for yourself), and a good-sized prudent reserve to tide you through the unpredictable spells of unemployment or underemployment that are so much more a part of your generation's lives than those of past generations.

On top of all of that, you are a human being, which just makes everything more complicated. Nobel Prize-winning behavioral economist Daniel Kahneman describes what he refers to as "system-1" versus "system-2" thought processes: human decision making is governed by a mashup of relatively newfangled brain areas where conscious thought and deliberation occur (system 2), and crusty old vestiges where snap judgments are made, weird cognitive errors occur, and emotions rule the roost (system 1). On the journey to financial success, system 2 is your friend. System 1? Well, not so much.

Take negotiations, for example, which play a huge role in financial success, from getting the salary you deserve, to bargaining on big-ticket purchases, to getting your credit card interest rate reduced. Most people know the time-honored wisdom of not being the first one to put a number on the table, because that first number gives your negotiating opponent valuable information about how much the deal is worth to you. But you can't even begin to imagine the havoc that that first number will wreak on your system-1 brain, should you be savvy enough to compel your opponent to go first. In an experiment at MIT, psychologist Dan Arielly asked MBA students to state how much a box of Belgian chocolates was worth to them in dollars. But first he asked them a question designed to focus their attention on the last two digits of their Social Security number, a purely random and irrelevant piece of information. Subjects with Social Security numbers ending in 80 or above valued the chocolates, on average, at $20. Those with final digits below 20 stated an average value of half that. That's a perfect example of what behavioral economists call "irrationality."

PRICE-SETTING JUST A FLUKE? How about Thomas Mussweiler and colleagues who asked a group of car dealers to put a value on a used car. Randomly, they told some of them that a friend had suggested the car was worth $5,000, and told others that the friend had said $2,800, numbers chosen to equal amounts above and below the independently assessed value of the car. The first group of subjects gave valuations an average of $1,000 higher than the second. A simple comment about the opinion of a friend affected the valuations of a set of experienced professionals by an average of a quarter of the assessed value of the car! And many of those were people who live and die by their negotiation skills.

You can try this kind of manipulation on your friends. It always works. It's just how our minds are wired. We are not fully rational decision makers. There is, however, some good news. In a lot of cases you can override your system-1 brain, and get yourself back onto solid, rational ground. In the used-car experiment, right after mentioning the so-called friend's opinion, Mussweiler and his colleagues asked some of their subjects to answer a simple question: "Tell me why this price might be too high (or low)?" Mechanics and dealers who were thus pulled back into their prefrontal cortex, and forced to engage in deliberative thought, gave the same valuations regardless of what initial "anchor" they'd been given. They were able to beat their system-1 brains.

Bottom line: you can make rational decisions if you know the pitfalls of your own mind and take the time to think things through. That's what this book is all about; the rational way to making decisions and achieving financial success. As a member of the Millennial Generation, you've got a myriad of financial decisions ahead of you, as well as habits of working, spending, borrowing, and saving to develop (or break). This book will give you road-ready knowledge of the world you are entering into and the strategies that will lead you to stability and success. But it will also help you develop the self-awareness to be able to identify and overcome the internal pitfalls that all of us (I promise you) are prone to.

THE POWER OF NOW   A group of subjects is randomly divided into two subgroups. The first group is asked, "Would you prefer $100 now or $105 in two weeks?" The second group is asked to choose between $100 in a year, and $105 in a year and two weeks. The results are always the same. Everyone in the second group is willing to wait an extra two weeks for an extra five bucks. But a large proportion of the first group (usually more than half) isn't. Why? Because $100 right now is *tempting*. There's just something special about *right now*! Not just special, but actually hard-wired. A team of researchers at Princeton put subjects into an fMRI machine, which is basically a massive magnet that makes a movie of the blood flowing through your brain. When a part of the brain gets activated, it receives more blood flow, which shows up as a red spot on the fMRI. Subjects were asked to make a series of decisions just like the $100/$105 setup above, except for real money. Always the later amount was bigger than the earlier amount, i.e. all the decisions involved choosing whether to be patient in order to earn a larger reward. But, as above, in some cases the early, smaller reward would be delivered immediately, as soon as the subject got out of the tank, while in others both the smaller and the larger reward were somewhere out in the future. The results were very striking, and confirmed the two-system hypothesis. When both rewards were in the future, only the rational, system-2 parts of the brain "lit up." But when the smaller, earlier reward was immediate, the irrational, system-1 parts lit up as well. And they lit up most powerfully when the subject actually gave in to temptation and chose the immediate reward. System 1 was driving impatient choices. Direct proof that there's a mechanism built into your brain that is custom-made to trip you up and make you do things you will later regret. Lots of things.

A favorite is to sign up for a credit card with a 0% "teaser rate" so you can buy some tempting shiny object, telling yourself you will pay it off before the rate jumps up to 21%. The logic seems to be, "I'm a tempted, "hyperbolic discounter" right now, but in a couple of months I'll be willing to resist temptation, tighten the belt, and pay off the card." The truth is, you're going to be the same person in a couple of months that you are right now, which means there's a good chance you'll succumb to temptation again, fail to pay off the card, and wind up accruing a whole lot of interest and regretting you ever signed up for the card in the first place. Behavioral economists refer to this kind of self-delusion as "naïveté," and it is responsible for all kinds of trouble. Naïveté is what makes people sign up for an expensive gym membership that they'll never use, and then procrastinate cancelling it, telling themselves over and over again that they'll cancel it tomorrow. It's what makes people take money out of their retirement savings, telling themselves they'll put it right back in as soon as they get their act together. And it's what makes people sit on the sofa flipping through other people's Pinterest boards, telling themselves that tomorrow they'll hit the pavement and find a job.

Now, you may or may not be that strongly affected by these traits, but we are all affected by them to some degree, and by plenty of other kinds of irrational mental processes as well. Whether you like it or not, you and your system-2 brain are going to spend a lifetime fighting against your system-1 brain. That is exactly where this book comes in. It will give you the strategy and the tactics for winning that fight. From negotiating your salary to planning for retirement to making a budget and sticking to it, this book will tell you *exactly* how to make rational, system-2 decisions, and help you to develop the habits and practices that will put those decisions into effect.

INTRODUCTION

This book won't tell you to separate your toilet paper plies to save fifty cents. And, if you want to learn how to spend thirty hours a week clipping coupons so that you can build a stockpile of processed foods and tooth-paste in your basement, there are other books that will serve you better. This is a book that will give you real-world, actionable information that you can actually implement with a view to making your life easier.

Ask any Millennial and they will agree that dealing with money is stressful, time consuming, and undoubtedly boring. It's with these readers in mind that this book was written. You will never catch me telling you to keep a budget journal on your person at all times, so you can diligently record every dollar you spend—and on what. Instead, you'll be advised to have a go at an app that tracks your payments and expenses, shows you your spending patterns and automates your budget keeping. This book melds tried-and-true strategies to get, or regain, control of your finances, with exciting new hacks to make everything as seamless as possible.

You might be wondering why we called it *Money* Is *Everything*. After all, Millennials are known to believe the exact opposite: that money *isn't* everything. Many of us will take jobs that give us flexibility and comfort over others that pay better. Making money may not be our top priority, but in order to achieve our dreams and live a fulfilling life, making and managing money successfully will become indispensable. Since we are so inclined to do amazing things, we need to get a very good grasp on making money work for us, spending more wisely, borrowing more intelligently and saving more efficiently; in short, maximizing our Return on Investment. We have structured this book accordingly, to take you through the entire cycle of money (from making to saving, via spending and borrowing) as effortlessly as possible.

Making It will show you how to get a coveted (and hopefully paid) internship, rock at your job, enjoy (and make good money) freelancing—and make a sizeable side income through our list of Side Hustles.

Spending It will take you through a step-by-step process for creating an awesome financial plan, budgeting like a pro, and saving money shopping. It will also go into detail about the big and important purchases in life, like cars, houses, and health insurance.

Borrowing It takes the perplexing world of credit scores, histories, and reports and boils it down to an easy-to-understand process that will give you access to better lines of credit, interest rates, and rewards. It will help you manage your personal credit, reduce your debt, slay your student loans, and make smart borrowing decisions.

Saving It will become your go-to guide for finding the smartest ways to take advantage of disposable income, show you when to save and when to pay off debt, and learn the fundamentals of investing.

Each section also features unique interviews with experts and real-world success stories, and a whole separate part called "Hacks," which will give you surprising, interesting, and practical information, like what sorts of practices you'd never think would increase your productivity.

I wrote this book to help you worry less about your future and your finances and focus more on the things that you like doing. So, read it, put the amazing advice to practice, and get on with life.

PART

MAKING IT

CHAPTER

INTERNSHIPS

So you've spent tens of thousands of dollars on a great education. Now it's time to go out into the world and work for *free*? Love them or hate them, internships are often a crucial step on the path toward adulthood and gainful employment. Whether they offer a reasonable salary, a stipend that barely covers your morning latte, or nothing at all, internships can provide experience crucial for landing a solid job. In this chapter, we'll explore ways to make the most out of internship opportunities and leverage them to get a paying gig.

PAID VS. UNPAID INTERNSHIPS

I know what you're thinking. Obviously, paid internships are better than unpaid opportunities. Actually, it depends on what you want to do and why you're doing an internship in the first place. Competition for paid internships is fierce, with Internships.com recording four times as many applications submitted for paid positions than unpaid ones. That means most students won't get one of those coveted spots.

In addition, there are simply no paid internships in some fields. Nonprofits and government organizations, for example, are exempt from the strict requirements that apply to unpaid internships. If you're out there trying to get experience in these fields or even just trying to get a better idea of whether or not they're right for you, you'll have a hard time if you limit yourself to only paid opportunities.

Still, unpaid internships are difficult, because you have to support yourself while you're working for free. While there are ways to make them work financially, make sure the benefits you'll reap from the experience will be worth the extra effort.

If you do take an unpaid internship, make sure it's legal. What many people don't know is that a for-profit company can't have unpaid interns do menial work like fetch coffees and make photocopies; this violates federal labor law. For a position to qualify as a legal unpaid internship, it must be explicitly for the benefit of the intern; the employer cannot derive immediate benefit; it has to offer training similar to the one given in an educational environment; and it should not displace other employees.

When it comes to paid versus unpaid internships, what really matters is if the opportunity is the right fit for you (see Table 1, page 20). Before you start your search, carefully think about why you want to intern; try to find the internship that will best fit your goals. Working all summer for free may actually help you find your dream job!

HOW TO FUND YOUR UNPAID INTERNSHIP

Internships can be great pathways to employment, but how do you support yourself while working for free?

Ask Your College Some colleges have internship funds or fellowships that can give you a little extra money to help you stay afloat during your unpaid internship.

Get a Second (Paying) Job Yes, you'll be working all the time; but this is how many interns make ends meet. Just put your shoulder to the wheel and think of your future.

Live at Home or with Roommates If it's possible, move back home with your parents or someone who can support you while you complete your internship. If that's not an option, find some other poor interns to bunk with. You'll save on rent and shared expenses either way.

INTERNSHIPS FOR COLLEGE CREDIT

While not all internships offer monetary compensation, there is one other way that some internships might pay you: in college credit. Still, not all schools offer credits for internships, and those that do often require that you pay tuition for the credits you get. Be sure to contact your school when you're applying for internships to find out how many credits you can get. Know what paperwork needs to be completed to ensure you get your credits.

While some schools limit the number of credits you can receive via internships, others only count unpaid internships. The Careers Office and your academic advisor are great sources of information on internships.

TABLE 1

WHAT TO LOOK FOR IN AN INTERNSHIP

The last thing you want to do is spend your summer working the internship from hell. Be sure to ask a lot of questions during your interview to get a clear idea of what the internship will be like, and try to ask other students who have completed the internship about their experiences.

THE PERFECT INTERNSHIP	THE INTERNSHIP FROM HELL
A major distinct project	Menial tasks
Clear mentorship	Little educational opportunity
Job opportunities	A company that isn't hiring
Relevance to your degree	A field you wouldn't work in when you graduate
Complex and interesting work	Not enough work or unclear expectations
Inclusion in the day-to-day	Exclusion from meetings
Enjoyable place to work	High stress or tense atmosphere
Reasonable hours with some overtime	Constant overtime
A reasonable salary	An unpaid internship

CAN YOU NEGOTIATE YOUR SALARY?

Suppose you get a salary offer for your internship—a very small offer. Miniscule, even. Is it negotiable?

While you *can* negotiate internship salaries, you might not be successful. Some companies have a set budget for interns, whereas others have more wiggle room. Your success (or lack thereof) will also depend on your field. If your field is one where qualified workers are in high demand, you'll have more leverage.

If you're offered an internship at a company that pays more than the one you want to work for, see if they can match the better offer. But remember to be reasonable about your demands. You might get a company offering an unpaid internship to give you a stipend, but you probably won't get them to give you a full salary.

If a salary increase isn't possible, consider asking for perks and other benefits. Companies may consider giving you a paid week off during the summer or offer you benefits usually reserved for full employees, like free parking or discounted gym memberships. For more tips on negotiating your salary, check out page 34 in the Jobs section.

COMPETITION FOR PAID INTERNSHIPS IS FIERCE, WITH *INTERNSHIPS.COM* REPORTING THAT THEY RECEIVE FOUR TIMES AS MANY APPLICATIONS FOR PAID POSITIONS THAN FOR UNPAID

OFFICE POLITICS!

Avoid the Drama Stay out of it. You don't want to be caught gossiping about your coworkers.

Know Your Place In school, professors want to hear what you think; once you enter the working world, you might find fewer people asking for your opinions. Companies are hierarchical organizations; as an intern, you're on the bottom rung. People higher on the ladder might feel like you're overstepping if you offer your unsolicited opinion on their projects. Spend a few days observing whether your employer encourages new hires or interns to give their opinions. If they do, speak up.

Build a Network The best way to navigate office politics is to make friends with other employees. Be friendly and thoughtful. Remember the names of people's kids and spouses and ask them questions about themselves.

WHAT ABOUT A JOB?

Some companies use their internship programs to test-drive future employees. It's a great way for companies to see if you're a good fit, without having to make the long-term commitment that comes with an official hire.

At the end of the summer, after having spent time and resources training you, it often makes more sense for a company to hire you instead of a complete stranger. But how do you make sure it's you they call, and not some other intern, when a position does become available? Here are some tips to increase your chances:

Fit into the Culture Companies take their culture very seriously these days. If everyone wears a suit every day, wear a suit. If people dress casually, do as they do. Participate in company activities and show enthusiasm. In short, embody the company's values.

ALTERNATIVES TO INTERNSHIPS

If an internship isn't in the cards, here are some other options to consider:

Co-operative Education Co-op programs offer the best of both worlds. They pay you, and you get college credit. Most schools have a co-op program that matches students up with paid work placements.

Volunteer Work You can get great experience when you volunteer—and you can build your commitments around your school or work schedule.

Work for Your Prof Professors hire students to help them do their research. Ask your profs if they are hiring. Working for a professor is a great way to get work experience.

Get a Cool Work-Study Job Work-study positions can range from the mundane to the fascinating. Get a work-study position that is applicable to your dream career.

Be Likeable Being sincere and pleasant plays a huge role in hiring decisions. Be the person that people want to work with. Show a genuine interest in your colleagues and get to know them. Be thoughtful. Make gestures that will endear you to coworkers.

Be Indispensable Some employees are skilled at making themselves indispensable. They always deliver spectacular work, even if it means staying late. They anticipate their bosses' needs. They never complain and always find a way to make it work. Be that indispensable person.

Act on Feedback While it can feel terrible to get negative feedback, try to see it as an opportunity. One of the hardest things to find is an employee who is adaptable. If someone gives you negative feedback, make the changes necessary to improve your work. You'll impress people by how quickly you learn.

Tell Them You Want to Work There Make sure your manager knows that you want to work there. Ask them to recommend you for other positions in the company if their department isn't currently hiring.

Get to Know Other Departments Reach out and build relationships with people from other departments. While the department you worked in might not be hiring when you need work, another department might be.

Ask Them to Recommend You to Others Maybe the company that you interned for isn't hiring. Ask your manager and colleagues to write recommendations on your LinkedIn profile. Ask them to let you know if they hear of openings at similar companies.

While internships can be great stepping-stones on the way to rewarding employment, they can also be tedious exercises. You need an internship to be a learning opportunity. Find out if there's a chance to be hired after the internship ends. Basically, don't sign up to just be someone's coffee-getter if you can avoid it.

WHAT'S IT REALLY LIKE TO BE AN INTERN?

What's it really like to be an intern? To find out, I talked to Emily Wight, a communications professional and the creator of the popular food blog *Well Fed, Flat Broke*. She did an internship in the publishing industry when she was in college and is now a published author.

FROM INTERNSHIP TO CAREER "I have worked since a month or two before my fifteenth birthday, and I worked pretty much full time throughout undergrad, so I have a lot of work experience, but I really wanted to have a meaningful career that I could enjoy and grow in—I needed a set of specific, employable skills. My internship was the beginning of a career in communications—the skills I learned in my internship have been applicable to my career. That experience was invaluable."

HER GRIPES "Dealing with (some) authors. Some writers are fiercely protective of their work. I remember getting pretty talked down to at one point for some changes I'd made copyediting someone's manuscript."

HER RAVES "I met a lot of fabulous people in the publishing industry, and a few of them are still very good friends. I hate to use the term 'networking,' but there really was a community that I enjoyed being a part of."

WHAT SHE LEARNED "I learned about editing and proofreading and about working with authors and 'subject matter experts,' which gave me the experience to move into a career in communications.

A GOOD INTERNSHIP "I have worked in places where an internship is just a form of free labor—those are not great opportunities. You need an internship to be a learning opportunity, and that's what an internship should be."

2
CHAPTER

JOBS

Unless your rich aunt left you a hefty inheritance, you'll need to work to support yourself. While more and more young people are freelancing or starting their own companies, the majority of Millennials will work traditional corporate jobs (see Figure 1). Millennials can expect to have up to twenty-five jobs over the course of their careers and spend an average of two to five years at each job.[1] In this chapter, we'll look at perfecting the art of landing a job and moving up the corporate ladder.

FIGURE 1

MILLENNIAL DOMINATION

PROJECTED PERCENTAGE OF
MILLENNIALS IN WORKFORCE

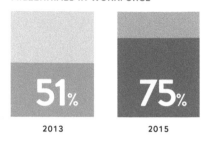

By 2015, Millennials will be the majority
of the workforce and by 2025, Millennials
will make up 75% of the workforce.

2013   2015

PERCENTAGE OF MILLENNIALS IN EXECUTIVE OR MANAGERIAL POSITIONS

Currently, 27% of Millennials are managers, with 5% in senior management and 2% in
executive positions. In the next 10 years, 47% of Millennials hope to be managers or
senior managers, 15% expect to be business owners, and 7% hope to be executives.

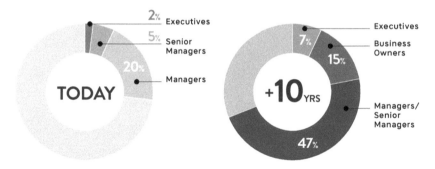

Source: The US Bureau of Labor Statistics Employment Projections, BPW Foundation, Elance-oDesk

GET AN INTERVIEW

The first step to getting a job is landing an interview, but that can some-times feel like an impossible goal. Anyone who has ever searched for a job knows the sinking feeling that comes with sending out resumes and not hearing anything back. Because of the high rates of unemployment and underemployment among Millennials, many companies are getting hundreds of applicants for each open position. How do you stand out from the herd in such an onslaught of resumes?

Network You might already have people in your network who can help you. Call them. Ask them to let you know if they hear of any opportuni-ties. Go to industry events and connect with influencers. Bring business cards listing your skills and contact information.

Contact people at companies or industries that you're interested in working for, and ask if they'll meet or take your call for an informational interview. You'll be surprised by how willing people are to meet with and help young job seekers. If you offer to treat them to coffee or lunch, you'll have their attention for 30 to 60 minutes. Use this time to find out more about their jobs and their companies, as well as to tell them a bit about yourself. Ask them to keep you in mind if there are openings in their departments.

If you've impressed them, they may give you a recommendation for a position at their company or connect you with an opportunity at another company. You're much more likely to get the job that way than by just shooting resumes into the dark.

Customize Your Resume The biggest mistake applicants make is sending the same resume to every potential employer. What you should do is spend at least an hour customizing your resume and cover letter to each job description. Highlight only the aspects of your experience that are relevant to the position. Use the same keywords that the job description uses. Spell out precisely why you're a perfect fit for this particular position.

WHY YOU NEED A PERSONAL BRAND

When it comes to the competitive job market, you need to stand out from others in your field with the same qualifications. How do you do that? The same way corporations have been standing out from their competitors for years: branding. The goal of personal branding is to define who you are and highlight why you're better than the competition. What traits do you have that you want employers to know about? You might want to emphasize your personality, how hard you work, or a rare skill you possess. Create a tagline on your resume that emphasizes that brand. When you're working, make sure that you act in a way that clearly reinforces your brand.

INTERVIEW LIKE A BOSS

Since statistics show[2] that Millennials will change jobs more often than Lady Gaga changes her outfit, interviewing is an important skill to have. An interview is an opportunity for an employer to get a sense of who you are and what you can contribute. The following tips will help you ensure that they see the value you would add to their team.

Prepare, Prepare, Prepare It's not difficult to guess the questions that you'll be asked. Most companies use standard interview questions; a quick Internet search will provide you with an abundance of practice questions. If you work in a field, like tech, where interviews are known to be intensive, preparation is even more crucial. It's not unheard of for candidates to undergo eight-hour interviews, complete with aptitude tests, oral presentations, panel interviews, and one-on-one interviews. For an advantage over the competition, visit sites like Glassdoor.com, where past applicants can post the actual interview questions companies ask.

Be Early Don't let roadwork, the search for parking, little old ladies crossing the road, or confusing directions keep you from getting to an interview on time. By planning to be absurdly early, you can eliminate the anxiety associated with arriving on time. This can keep you cool and collected and ensure you're in the right mindset when your interview starts.

Learn about the Company While you don't have to memorize the company's mission statement, you should have a detailed understanding of what they do and what their goals are. Do a Google News search to see if they've been in the news recently and why. Familiarize yourself with their products or services and their company culture. Show enthusiasm for what they do and anticipate what their next steps might be.

Dress for Success Some hiring managers assume that Millennials are immature or irresponsible because they're young (see Table 2 for how to deal with stereotypes). Dress for the job you want. Not only will looking good give you confidence, but it makes you look mature and polished. While you should put effort into looking good for your interview, keep in mind where you'll be working.

TABLE 2
HOW TO DEAL WITH STEREOTYPES

Millennials have gotten a bad reputation in the workplace. I think it's undeserved and that a few bad eggs have ruined it for the rest of us. But as you head out into the working world, you should know how you might be stereotyped and what you can do to counteract it.

THE STEREOTYPE	HOW TO HANDLE IT
We're entitled	Show that you're willing to work hard for whatever you get
We're not loyal	Don't jump from job to job. Try to stay at jobs for two to three years
We don't work hard	Make it a point to work harder than everyone else
We waste time on social media or texting	Don't text or log into social media during work hours
We can't take negative feedback	Seek out negative feedback to help you improve

Ask the Right Questions The biggest mistake that candidates make when interviewing is not asking questions when given the opportunity to do so. The second biggest mistake candidates make is to ask about salary first when they're given a chance to ask a question. Show employers that you're seriously interested in working for their businesses by asking insightful questions.

Be Confident Don't let anything throw you off during your interview. It's not over until the interviewer tells you he or she has given the job to someone else.

CHOOSE THE RIGHT OPPORTUNITY

If you find yourself with more than one job offer, how do you choose among an embarrassment of riches? While salary and benefits will play an important role in your decision, there are a few other factors you should weigh when deciding.

1. Consider which position will give you the best chance to gain the experience you need to move to the next stage of your career. Take into account in-house opportunities for advancement. If one job provides you with more responsibility or opportunities, it might make sense to choose that job.

2. Think about what your work-life balance and quality of life will be in each position. If one job would require you to work a lot of overtime you don't want to work, that might help you choose. See Figure 2 for flexibility in the workplace.

3. Next, look carefully into the companies. If one company culture is a better fit for your personality or working style, that might help you make your decision. Also, if one company has a great reputation or is an industry leader, working for that company will reflect well on you later in your career.

FIGURE 2

FLEXIBILITY AT WORK

The majority of Millennial workers are looking for flexibility at work, but how many employers truly offer it?

PREVALENCE OF FLEXIBILITY PROGRAMS SORTED BY EMPLOYEE COVERAGE

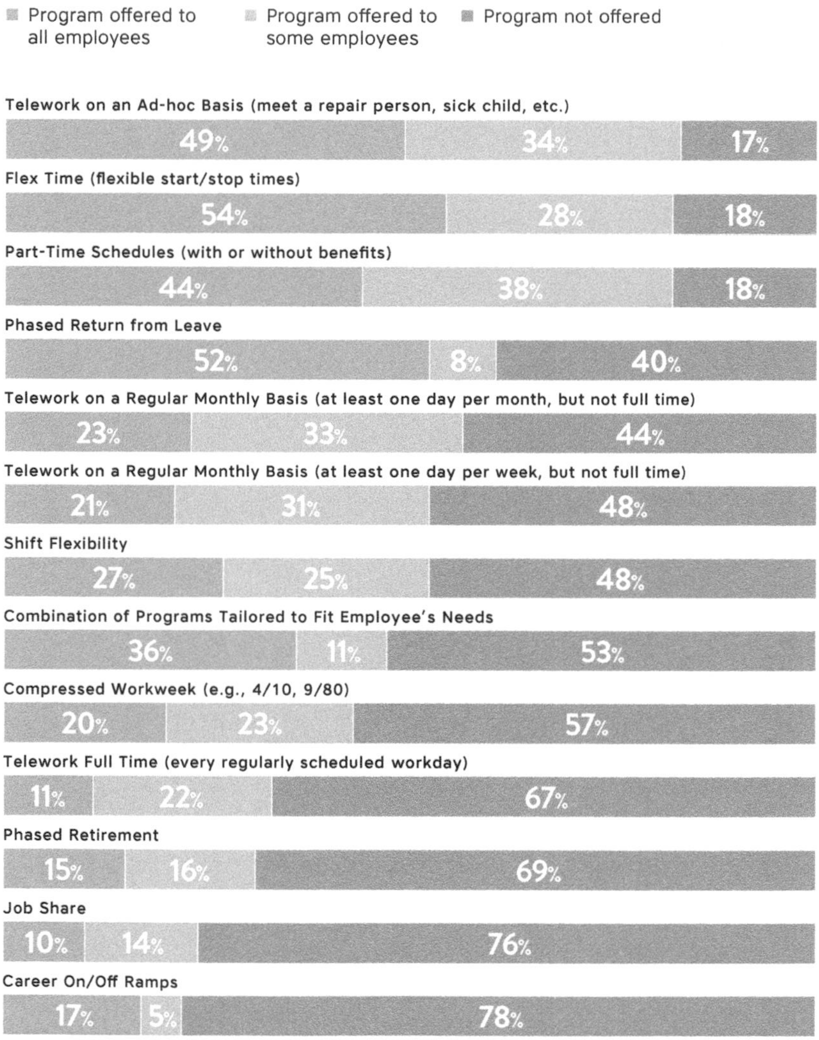

■ Program offered to all employees ■ Program offered to some employees ■ Program not offered

Telework on an Ad-hoc Basis (meet a repair person, sick child, etc.)

| 49% | 34% | 17% |

Flex Time (flexible start/stop times)

| 54% | 28% | 18% |

Part-Time Schedules (with or without benefits)

| 44% | 38% | 18% |

Phased Return from Leave

| 52% | 8% | 40% |

Telework on a Regular Monthly Basis (at least one day per month, but not full time)

| 23% | 33% | 44% |

Telework on a Regular Monthly Basis (at least one day per week, but not full time)

| 21% | 31% | 48% |

Shift Flexibility

| 27% | 25% | 48% |

Combination of Programs Tailored to Fit Employee's Needs

| 36% | 11% | 53% |

Compressed Workweek (e.g., 4/10, 9/80)

| 20% | 23% | 57% |

Telework Full Time (every regularly scheduled workday)

| 11% | 22% | 67% |

Phased Retirement

| 15% | 16% | 69% |

Job Share

| 10% | 14% | 76% |

Career On/Off Ramps

| 17% | 5% | 78% |

Source: World at Work from the Survey on Workplace Flexibility 2013[3]

4. Be careful if you find out one of the companies is in a precarious financial position; this might mean layoffs in the future. Since many companies follow the "last in, first out" rule, your new job could be in danger.

5. If you know someone who works at any of the companies you're considering, ask that person what it's like to work there. Ask him or her why the person who had the position you've been offered left. This connection will give you an insider's perspective, which might be just what you need to make your decision.

6. If you're still not sure, add up all the factors and compare the various opportunities. If there is no clear winner, trust your gut. You might have unconsciously picked up on something important during the interview that would impact your experience working there.

NEGOTIATE YOUR SALARY

Many Millennials accept the first salary amount a company offers them. That's a big mistake. That first offer is just the beginning of a conversation. In most jobs, you can negotiate for a higher salary and better benefits. It turns out HR departments often purposely authorize a low initial salary offer but have extra money to offer an applicant if he or she asks for it.

Negotiating for a higher salary can feel risky. Still, if the company has offered you a job, it means they value you. Nobody wants to hire the second-best candidate or have to start the candidate search all over again. Your value to them, and their need for someone to fill the position quickly, is the leverage you have in the negotiation. Very few people have had a job offer revoked because they negotiated their salary.

Determine a Fair Salary Young workers sometimes have a hard time determining what they're worth. You have to do your research. Find out what the industry standard is for a position like yours in your city. Once you've settled on a reasonable salary range, determine what you would like to get and what you need to get within that range. What you want to get is an aspirational number that might not be possible—but one you will still ask for. What you need to get is the minimum that you're willing to accept to do the job.

Bring Other Offers If you have another job offer, be honest about how much the other company has offered you. Explain that you would rather work for their company and that you hope they can meet or exceed your other offer. Knowing everything you can about the other company's offer, including things like benefits, will help you negotiate a fair deal.

Be Confident Negotiating your starting salary can be stressful. If you really need or really want the job, it can feel reckless not to accept the first salary offer. But remember that, after an exhaustive search, they have chosen you. In a confident manner, make the case for why they should pay you more to work for them; they will often be impressed.

Get Better Benefits Benefits—including health plans, 401(k)s, parental leaves, and a host of others—make up a significant part of your total compensation package and need to factor into the negotiation process. Learn as much as you can about the benefits your potential employer provides. Know how they differ from your current job or any other job offers. If the benefits aren't great, try to get the company to make up for them by paying you more. Also, if the company can't meet your salary number, consider negotiating for more vacation days. Once you've agreed on terms, make sure that you get the job offer in writing.

HOW TO BE A SUPERSTAR EMPLOYEE

Once you have the job, you need to prove to an employer that he or she made a good choice in hiring you. If you want to move up the corporate ladder and get a raise every year, your mission should be to come as close to being a perfect employee as possible. That might mean doing last-minute assignments that will keep you at the office when you would much rather be at the bar with friends or home with family. It might also mean supporting your boss and not speaking out against company policies (even if everyone thinks they are dumb). Here are some tips to help you become a superstar in your office.

Be a Problem Solver Some people like to complain about things, but either they aren't able or willing to come up with solutions. If there is a problem, don't complain publicly about it; tell your boss privately. Suggest at least one solution and you'll come across as someone who is resourceful.

Work Independently The ability to work independently is especially important if you want a chance to move up in your company. When you get assigned a project, be sure to ask all the questions you need to ask upfront. Being good at working independently, however, also involves knowing when to ask for more information. If something crucial comes up that you hadn't anticipated, speak to your boss about it.

Show Leadership Offer to be the lead on a big project or volunteer to stay late to finish a project. Set a good example for others; this will help your boss see you in a leadership position in the future.

Find a Mentor Sometimes success at work is less about what you know than who you know. Finding a mentor in senior management might greatly improve your chances of moving up. Some companies have formal mentorship programs that pair junior and senior employees. If your company doesn't, ask someone to informally mentor you. Invite them out for lunch to get their advice on how to successfully build a career within the company.

Ask for More Work and Responsibility When some people finish the work assigned to them, they're afraid to ask for more because it might show that there isn't enough work to justify their position. By asking for more work, however, you show that you work quickly and do a good job.

Be Positive No one wants to work with someone who is always pessimistic or downcast. Be friendly and positive and your colleagues will be happy to help you succeed.

Get Clear Expectations Ask your boss for clear yearly or quarterly milestones or metrics that you can strive toward. Many bosses will be impressed that you've taken the initiative to ask. By having clear metrics, you have quantitative evidence that you've done your job when your annual review comes up.

HOW TO ASK FOR A PAY RAISE

After you've worked at your job for a while, you might think that you've contributed enough to the company's bottom line to merit a pay raise. You just need to convince your boss that you're worth it. Follow these suggestions to increase your chances of scoring a pay bump.

Make a Strong Case Create a document listing everything that you've accomplished since you were hired. If you're in a sales position, include your sales figures. If you've been in charge of any major projects, be sure to list each project's accomplishments. If you have great performance reviews, mention those. When you approach your boss to ask for a raise, give them this document. If they need to think it over, this document will hopefully help convince them.

Pick the Right Time By choosing the right time to ask for a raise, you're more likely to be successful. For example, if you approach your boss after you've scored a big win for your team, your value to the company will be at the top of his or her mind. Don't choose a time when your boss is stressed out or when there is uncertainty around some aspect of your company's future. If your company only gives raises during your annual review, wait until then; if not, choose a time when your boss will be primed to say yes.

Make a Reasonable Request If you can, find out the average size of raises in your company. Once you have an idea of what might be possible, approach your boss and make your case. Tell your boss the figure you have in mind. If they aren't able to meet your expectations, accept what they can give you. If you feel you're now worth more than they can offer, consider looking for a job that will value you properly. See Table 3 for info about Millennial salary ranges.

SOME PEOPLE THINK THAT THE BEST WAY TO GET A RAISE IS TO BRING ANOTHER OFFER TO THE TABLE, BUT THIS MIGHT BACKFIRE

TABLE 3
AVERAGE INCOME FOR MILLENNIALS

AGE BRACKET	2013 INCOME
15 to 24 years	$34,311
25 to 34 years	$52,702

Source: www.advisorperspectives.com[4]

Ask for a Promotion Since you're asking for more money, consider also asking for more responsibility. If you've contributed enough to justify a change in your work title or if there are new responsibilities that you could potentially take on, consider asking for a promotion in addition to a raise.

TRANSITIONING TO A NEW JOB

There are many reasons why you might be looking for another job. Maybe your coworkers are insufferable, your job description is a joke, and your boss has anger issues. Or perhaps your current job is just a bad fit for your skill set and career goals. Whatever the reason, be careful how you manage the transition process to ensure that you don't burn bridges or end up jobless.

Keep It to Yourself We all have work friends who we trust with the personal details of our lives. While you might bond by talking about how unreasonable Janet from HR is, you don't want to take the chance that they might slip and say something about your plans. The fact that you're interviewing elsewhere is juicy news. If they tell the wrong person, you could be in trouble. Some managers will even fire you if they hear that you're trying to leave, because they don't see you as loyal anymore. No matter how much you might want to talk about it, you're better off keeping it to yourself until you have a job offer from another company.

FIGURE 3

THE SOCIAL MEDIA NETWORKS MOST USED IN JOB SEARCHES

Make sure your social media accounts are up-to-date and career-oriented and they just might help you land a job.

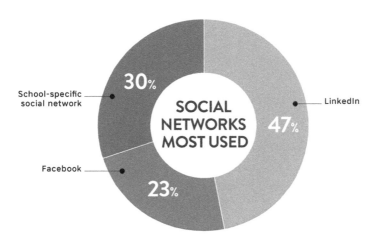

Wait Until You Have Your Next Job While you might be tempted to quit your job if it's insufferable, try to stick it out until you find your next position. It's tough to keep working in an environment that you've decided you want to leave, but you're better off collecting a paycheck while you're searching.

Network If you've been in your current position for a while, your professional network outside your company might have grown stale. If that's the case, get out and network with other people within your industry. Don't openly tell people that you're looking for a new job, but confidentially contact new connections if an opportunity comes up in their company.

Leave on a Positive Note While you might be tempted to quit by creating a dramatic YouTube video that details the various injustices you have experienced while working at a certain company, you're much better off taking the high road. Sure, you'll miss the gratification of finally telling everyone what you think about them, but you also won't get a bad name that will haunt you for the rest of your career. The people you're currently working with will most likely spread out to different companies in your field, possibly making it more difficult for you in the future. The best way to leave a job is to do it in a way that the company would hire you again if ever given the chance.

Be Careful With References References are the job seeker's catch-22. You don't want your boss to know that you're looking for a new job, but you need someone to be your reference. Try to get a former boss to act as your reference. Some companies have a policy that require them to speak with your current manager or someone who has worked with you in your current position. If that's the case, ask them if they can hold off on checking references until you're the final candidate. That way you're far more likely to get the job by the time you have to tell your boss you're leaving.

HOW DO YOU BUILD A GREAT REPUTATION AT WORK?

Candy Ho works as a university instructor, teaching an eight-week course for co-operative education students. She also runs a career-consulting business called *Career Connections Consulting*. In this section, she shares her secrets with you.

WHAT HELPED HER GET HER FIRST JOB? "I did co-operative education while I was in school, which was great because I was able to get paid, hands-on work experience. Right before I graduated, my co-op supervisor hired me for a front-counter position in student services. When I took co-op, I was told a high percentage of students who work in the co-op program would end up working for their employer. I was certainly one of those statistics."

HOW DID SHE MANAGE TO BUILD SUCH A GREAT REPUTATION? "I remember a former boss telling me that I have a can-do attitude. Right from the beginning, I treated my job as a career. In every position I've taken on, I've always thought about how I could add value to the organization. You need to make yourself the CEO of your own organization. I'm the Chief Executive Officer of *Candy, Inc*. I'm responsible for the marketing department, the day-to-day administration, and how I present myself. That means I work hard doing things like making sure that I do my homework before going into meetings so that I can add something constructive, and being careful about how I present myself on Facebook and LinkedIn."

WHY SHOULD YOU CONDUCT INFORMATIONAL INTERVIEWS? "If you're at a stage where you don't yet know what you want to do, you should start talking to people you admire and conduct informational interviews. This will help give you an idea of whether or not you're interested in someday doing a job like theirs. Always ask them if they know other people they can recommend you talk to."

HOW DO YOU GET PROMOTED? "On your very first day at your job, you need to start thinking about the future and planning for your next step. You might not know what it is yet, but it's that mindset that will help you create a positive impression. In your first month you should take the initiative to meet with your supervisor and ask them for feedback to make sure you're on the right track. The other thing you need to start doing right away is fitting into the culture. Join the social committee and get involved in planning fun things for your office that will keep the morale high. It's a great way to meet people from different departments, which could lead to opportunities."

HOW CAN MILLENIALS GET A COMPETITIVE EDGE IN THE WORKFORCE? "In order to move up in the world you need to work beyond the 9 to 5. You might need to work 7 to 7. You need to be able to show that you're hard-working and that you've got a strong work ethic in order. In addition, you have to leverage the skills you bring. Assets that Millennials often bring to workplaces are adaptability and innovation. For my parent's generation the emphasis was on knowledge and management was pretty top down. But in this day and age, there's more of a dynamic exchange of knowledge up and down and organizational hierarchies. I'm beginning to see senior administrator recognize the talents that Millennials bring to the workplace and take the initiative to learn from them.

I've seen increases in co-op student employment since companies like the new and fresh perspective co-op students give. For many of these businesses, Millennials are going to be their biggest customers. So, they often hire more Millennials to be part of their operation to give that perspective."

WHAT IS THE MOST IMPORTANT SKILL THAT MILLENNIALS NEED TO SUCCEED? "I hear over and over again that skills can be trained. Companies are willing to teach you but it's the attitude that matters. You need to show them that you're willing to do the job, to learn, and to fit into the company culture. That is the key to succeeding in the workplace."

3
CHAPTER

SELF-EMPLOYMENT AND FREELANCING

Want to work in your pajamas? If you decide to freelance or start your own business, your dream just might come true. While self-employment can offer you more flexibility and greater control over your work than a position with a company, it also means you'll have less certainty about when you'll get paid and more stress over acquiring clients. If you can handle the unpredictability, this chapter will show you what you need to succeed at self-employment.

HOW TO START YOUR OWN BUSINESS

Just like a car takes a while to go from 0 to 60, don't expect to start off your freelancing career at full speed. Unfortunately, there is no freelancing fairy to build up a client base for you and get you paid on time. Here are a few things that will help you get started.

Decide Where You Want to Specialize Perhaps you've done social media marketing and want to provide social media management and consulting services. That's a pretty broad field. If you narrow your focus and find a niche or two to specialize in, then you're more likely to be seen as an expert within a particular business community and more likely to have customers come to you. For example, you might focus your social media business on restaurants.

Learn Your Market If you're offering a service to businesses, be sure to focus on small- or medium-size businesses that can't afford to hire an expert in-house. If you're offering a service to consumers, find a niche that isn't well-served in your area. For example, if you want to tutor, consider focusing on a subject or age group for which there are fewer tutors in your area.

Give a Discount When you're pitching to new clients, they may want to see your past work or even talk to former clients. Offer your services for free or at a discount to secure some testimonials. This trial run will also help you refine and perfect your service.

Brand Yourself Whatever the market, if you want to succeed you have to stand out. One of the ways to do that is to brand yourself. Give your freelance company a name and create a tagline. Your name tells potential clients about the particular areas in which you specialize. Figure out what is unique about the services that you offer and highlight that in your branding. Ensure that whatever name you choose isn't used by anyone else, so people will be able to easily find you online.

Go the Extra Mile Make sure that your first clients are happy with your work by giving them a little something extra. That might mean

WHY MILLENNIALS CHOOSE TO WORK FOR THEMSELVES

Trina Isakson of *27 Shift* spoke about her reason for becoming a free-lancer: "Having control over my schedule and the work that I take on was important to me. I don't like maintaining programs; I like building them. As a consultant, I can focus on that." She realizes that for many Millennials becoming a freelancer is not a choice: "It's just the nature of the job market right now. Many employers aren't wanting to hire full-time employees and so they turn to freelancers." But she offers this advice to those who are freelancing out of necessity: "One good thing about freelancing is that it gives you the ability to try out different kinds of work and different employers. This gives you a better sense of who you would want to work with if you ever do want a job."

doing some extra work for one of your bigger clients or doing something thoughtful. Little gifts like chocolates don't cost much but do leave people with a warm feeling. Also, give your clients the opportunity to provide feedback in order to continually improve your service.

Ease into It If you have a full-time job, consider keeping it until you build your freelancing career to the point where there is enough business to replace your income. If you quit your job without first building up a client base, you may struggle to make enough money to pay your bills.

MARKET YOURSELF

If you've branded yourself well, you've already done half the work of mar-keting yourself. Now you need to find a way to tell people how amazing you are. While it can be uncomfortable to toot your own horn, if you're a freelancer who likes to eat and have a home to sleep in, you're going to need to find a way to get over that. Here are some suggestions for how to attract customers:

Create Great Marketing Materials Get a graphic designer to help you build a professional-looking website, logo, proposal template, and business cards. Add samples of your work and testimonials to your website. Make sure to include a bio and a pitch for your services.

Build Your Social Media Profile Create social media profiles on the sites that are relevant to your industry. Develop a reputation for being an expert by sharing quality content and engaging with others in your industry.

Write an E-book Want to be seen as an expert? Consider writing an e-book and giving it away for free. It doesn't have to be hundreds of pages long. It can be short and sweet, so long as it provides quality content. Choose a topic relevant to your clients and connected to the services you provide. Offer it for free on your website, Amazon.com, or other sites that host e-books.

Go to Industry Events Face-to-face marketing is the most effective kind of marketing. You can pitch potential clients on your services right there or ask them for a follow-up meeting. Get business cards so you can follow up with anyone you think has the potential to become a client. Conferences, networking nights, and industry lunches are great for this type of networking.

Consider Content Marketing Content marketing is when companies create content like videos, blog posts, or social media posts in order to attract potential customers to their brands online. It's so successful that all the big companies have adopted content marketing strategies. If you start a blog about problems or issues that are of interest to your clients, you can bring potential clients to your website and get them to subscribe to your newsletter. If they find the content you provide valuable, they will be more likely to hire you in the future.

Get Your Clients to Market for You Happy clients are the best marketers for your business. Ask them to recommend you to anyone who they think might benefit from your services. Consider also providing them with discounts or credits if they refer someone who hires you.

HOW TO STAY MOTIVATED

It can be difficult for many people to stay motivated when they're working from home. The first thing you need to do is create structure by developing a schedule for yourself. Decide which hours you'll spend working and make sure that you have clear objectives for what you expect to accomplish during those periods. Other tips to help you be productive include getting out of your pajamas, working in a dedicated office area, rewarding yourself for completing tasks, alternating your projects, and regularly engaging with other people to fight the loneliness.

The Elevator Pitch What can you say to catch a potential client's attention in the time it takes to ride in an elevator—before the doors open and they're gone forever? Keep your elevator pitch short and sweet and make sure it tells someone why you're unique and why they should hire you.

Cold Call In a high-tech world, cold calling is still an effective way to get business. Whether you make actual calls or send out targeted emails, you need to remember that it's a numbers game. The more people you connect with, the greater the likelihood one of them will be interested in your services.

FEE STRUCTURES

Determining what to charge when freelancing can be difficult. You might easily be able to calculate the hourly rate you received at your last job, but that won't include the cost of all the benefits that you received or the overhead you'll pay as a freelancer.

To calculate a reasonable freelance rate, some experts suggest doubling the amount you made per hour working in that field for a company. Other people suggest figuring out how much money you want to end up with at the end of the year, factor in your business and added personal expenses from freelancing, and divide that by the number of billable hours you expect to work. Keep in mind that some of your time will be spent seeking and soliciting business; you may not be able to work 40 hours a week for clients.

Because of the uncertainty surrounding getting stable work, you might want to take whatever number you arrive at and tack on a little bit extra as insurance against uncertainty.

Benefits of Charging by the Hour Charging by the hour ensures that you get the wage you need to make the project worthwhile while still giving a competitive price to your client.

Benefits of Charging a Flat Fee There are a lot of benefits to charging a flat fee for your services, both for you and your clients. For one, clients tend to prefer paying a flat fee because they can more easily budget for it.

BUILD A STEADY INCOME STREAM

There are a lot of ways to build a steady income stream as a freelancer. The most obvious way is to get one or two major clients to pay you the majority of your annual salary. Of course, if it was that easy, everyone would be doing it! While it can be difficult to build the relationships that lead to large contracts, you can reap huge benefits by doing so. When you have large clients you don't have to spend as much time soliciting new clients, letting you concentrate on working billable hours and getting paid.

Still, many freelancers work in fields where it's impossible to get a major client to pay a significant chunk of their annual salaries. These freelancers might find more stability by offering packages to their clients. By providing a volume discount, clients may purchase more hours of their time. These clients are locked into working with the freelancers and can potentially provide the freelancers with more revenue than they might have gotten if they had continued to work on an hourly basis. The best thing about volume discounts is that clients pay you ahead of time, so you aren't waiting to finish the job to get your money.

Another way of building a steady income stream as a freelancer is to provide clients with subscriptions. If you are doing social media management for restaurants, you might offer a monthly package that includes daily account monitoring, a commitment to expand their followers by a certain number, and a few posts, tweets, and Instagram pictures a week. If you charge $500 per month for this service and have 15 clients, you'll make $7,500 a month just on subscriptions alone. By creating a subscription instead of charging for a flat fee for each service, you'll ensure that you get paychecks on a monthly basis.

WHERE TO WORK

One of the benefits of freelancing is being able to work from home. But that's also one of its drawbacks. Coworkers are one of the best parts of working for a company. Getting out of the house is another benefit of having a conventional job. Some people go crazy if they spend every day working at home, while others have trouble staying motivated. Here are some options for other places to work:

A Rented Office If you need to meet frequently with clients or you like having some place to go every day that you can call your own, it might make sense for you to rent an office. This is particularly useful if you work closely with other people or if your work equipment isn't mobile. To cut costs, you might consider sharing space with other freelancers in need of an office.

A Coffee Shop It's a cliché for a reason. Buy a coffee and most shops will let you type away at your computer with access to their free Wi-Fi for hours. If you get hungry or thirsty, there is food right there. I love ambient noise when working, so coffee shops are ideal for me.

A Library If you prefer a quiet place to work, consider the public library. I love working in libraries, especially college libraries because they tend not to have young children running around. Find a library that offers Wi-Fi and a cozy nook to plug in your laptop and work.

A Coworking Hub With the rising number of freelancers and startups, there is a growing need for spaces for client meetings or work during the day. Coworking spaces meet those needs in a flexible manner. A coworking space allows freelancers or startups to rent working space, conference rooms, mailboxes, and other amenities on a daily, weekly, or monthly basis. Not only are you able to pay only for the space you use when you use it, but you also get to be part of a community of people just like you. Many people who use coworking spaces find that one of the benefits is the ability to network and potentially find new clients.

HOUSEKEEPING FOR FREELANCERS

A whole host of things that are more or less taken care of for you when you work for an established organization fall squarely on the shoulders of freelancers. Money management, planning for retirement, and a certain legal structure are just a few. Here are a few tips to help you stay ahead of the paperwork and plan for the future.

Separate Your Accounts To keep things simple, set up a business account. Deposit all checks and pay all business expenses from that account. This will make your business accounting much simpler. Consider buying software or signing up for a service that allows you to easily keep track of your cash flow and payments. See Table 4 for apps that make running your business easier.

Have an Emergency Fund Since you don't have the certainty of a regular paycheck, the comfort of a robust emergency fund can help. Make sure you have enough money to cover your bills for anywhere from three to six months. This will help you deal with the cash flow issues that most freelancers experience.

TABLE 4
APPS FOR RUNNING YOUR BUSINESS

APP	WHAT IT DOES
Wave Accounting	This app helps you manage your accounting and create and send invoices.
Shoeboxed	This app helps you organize receipts and track your expenses or mileage.
Timely	This app helps you keep your schedule straight, book meetings with clients, and keep track of how many hours you work on different projects.
Mozy	Many freelancers get paid for documents and project files. Make sure you back them up on a cloud storage service like Mozy so that you don't lose all your work.

Don't Forget Your Taxes Taxes can be a nightmare as a freelancer. Since you don't have an employer to figure out and withhold the amount you owe in taxes, you need to do this on your own. Some freelancers keep their taxes in a separate account to make sure the money is there when it comes time to pay Uncle Sam. It's better to be safe than have the IRS after you.

Make Your Health a Priority When you're working for yourself, you don't get the benefit of a company health plan. If you're relatively healthy, you might be tempted to buy a cheap plan. But what happens if you get into an accident or get sick? You could end up thousands of dollars in debt. It's not worth it. Get a real plan and consider starting a health savings account (HSA), allowing you to save money tax-free to pay for qualified medical expenses.

Get Disability Insurance If you do get sick, you might not be able to work, which means you won't have any income. Unlike working a conventional job, you don't get sick days as a freelancer. Make sure you get disability insurance to help you cope if you're unable to work for a significant period of time. If you don't, you could end up in a terrible financial position.

Don't Neglect Your Retirement Just because you aren't working for a company doesn't mean you can neglect your retirement savings. You might think that since you're young you can make up for not saving now later on. By investing now, you'll benefit from compound interest.

Set Up Payment Plans for Clients One of the problems with doing large freelance contracts is that some clients want to pay you half up front and half on delivery. A contract that is a one year long makes it difficult to manage your money while you're waiting six months for the other half of your year's salary. Instead, try to set up a monthly or bimonthly payment plan. Some may request that you set up milestones where you deliver certain parts of the work in exchange for payment. This strategy also helps protect you against clients not paying or sending your payment late.

Carefully Manage Your Cash Flow Have a clear idea of what your expenses will be each month, as well as when you can expect payments from clients. If you have big purchases coming up, make sure you'll have enough clients paying you that month to be able to cover the costs.

Take Care of the Legal Stuff Of huge importance for your legal standing is business registration. You'll need to register your business name, obtain any business licenses or permits required, get a tax ID number, and register for state and local taxes. If you plan on having employees, you should make sure you understand the legal responsibilities you will have to them as an employer. These tasks are highly bureaucratic and not a lot of fun, but they're necessary to get to the part where you're running your own, legitimate business.

SOME FREELANCERS CHARGE HIGHER FLAT FEES TO OFFSET THE LACK OF CONSTANT PROJECTS

Invest Back into Your Skills When you're working for an employer, they will often send you to go to conferences or to take special courses to expand your skill set. When you're working for yourself, you should set aside money each year to do the same. Think carefully about things that would help your business. Maybe you currently pay someone to do rudimentary graphic design work like editing photos or making infographics. If so, learning Photoshop might save you money. Perhaps an additional credential or course might allow you to raise your hourly rate or make your services be in more demand. Just as if you were working at a job, you need to consider how you can move to the next stage of your career. Develop a two- to three-year plan for your professional growth and choose your professional development activities accordingly.

WHAT'S IT REALLY LIKE TO FREELANCE?

If you're considering becoming a freelancer (or if you are one already), it can help to hear advice from people who have been freelancing for years. Nik Parks is cofounder of the popular blog *Launching Creative* and host of the *Launching Creative* podcast. His mission is to help creative freelancers become business-savvy professionals. Nik has the following to say:

WHY HE STARTED FREELANCING "Full disclosure: freelancing was a last resort for me. I never saw myself as a freelancer when I was studying graphic design in college. However, I've learned along the way that freelancing is a wonderful career path and it most certainly is not a last resort.

As Millennials, we've all felt the impact of the slow economic recovery. Businesses are trimming expenses in order to maximize profits. One of the ways they are doing this is by outsourcing to freelancers instead of hiring full-time employees."

HIS CHALLENGES "One of the biggest challenges is knowing how to price yourself. Let's face it, talking about money is scary and uncomfortable—especially when you're the one making the demands. I've gone through all of the emotions of pricing myself: panicking because I don't know what to say, throwing out a low price so the client won't get mad, feeling like an idiot for selling myself short, etc.

Setting your own deadline is also a big struggle. As a freelancer, you need to remember three things:

1. Be honest with yourself. No client likes a freelancer who over-promises and under-delivers.

2. Ask a lot of questions at the beginning. The more you know about the project upfront, the more accurate your estimate will be on your price and on meeting the deadline.

3. Don't assume the client is mad. If the client is unhappy, they'll let you know."

THE PROS AND CONS OF FREELANCING "There are many advantages to freelancing. You can establish your own hours, the market doesn't dictate your potential income the way it dictates an employee's salary, and you get to enjoy a lot of freedom. You can also have multiple streams of income.

There are, however, some drawbacks too. It can get exceptionally lonely, especially if you work from home. You don't have a consistent income. And you're probably going to experience some occasional slow seasons. You also have to spend a lot of time on unbillable hours spent networking, marketing, invoicing, and doing other things."

TABLE 5

PROS	CONS
Freedom to plan your day	Potential to overwork or procrastinate
Make more money per hour	Potential to make less overall
A variety of projects	Risk of not being paid
You might be happier	No health care or other benefits
No commute	Loneliness
Choice of what you do	Slow times without clients

HIS ADVICE TO THOSE STARTING OUT "Word of mouth is crucial. I can watch a movie trailer 100 times, but I won't necessarily be compelled to pay money to see the movie in theaters. However, if one of my close friends tells me that I will love the movie, I'm going to watch the movie.

If you can get your clients to tell their inner circle about you, your business will grow. How do you do this? Show an exceptional work ethic, meet their deadlines, be pleasant (that's a really important one), and fix your mistakes quickly."

CHAPTER

SIDE HUSTLES

Why waste your free time watching TV when you could use it to make money? Whether you have enormous student loans you want gone or you're saving for something special, a side hustle might be just what you need. It could be a second job, an entrepreneurial venture, an artistic project, or part-time consulting work. This chapter will help you figure out if you need a side hustle, give you some great ideas for side hustles, and provide tips to get you started.

EMBRACE THE SHARING ECONOMY

What's the sharing economy? It's the modern equivalent of your neighbor asking to borrow your lawnmower—only you don't know the person and they pay you to borrow it. In terms of a side hustle, it's a great way to make extra cash off things you already own. What can you rent out and make money on?

Your Space Sites like Airbnb.com allow you to rent out a room in your house (or your whole house) for the night, the week, or the month. Airbnb requires potential guests to set up a profile and have references. You can choose to accept a guest or not based on whether you think they're a good fit. A word of caution: if you're a renter, be careful not to violate the terms of your lease by renting out your space, or you could find yourself evicted. DogVacay.com is another way you can monetize your home. For dog owners, it's a great alternative to leaving their pet at the kennel when they go away.

Your Car If you have a decent car, you can use it to make money. Companies like Lyft.com and Uber.com allow you to drive people around to earn extra dough. Other companies like RelayRides.com and Getaround.com allow you to rent your car out to strangers. If you don't mind a stranger driving your car, you can make a lot of money that way.

Your Bike Spinlister.com allows you to rent out your bike by the week, the day, or the hour. Earn some extra money while you're not pedaling around.

Your Money LendingClub.com allows you to lend people your money. Instead of getting a loan or using credit cards, borrowers can access lower interest rates through Lending Club. For lenders, you get better interest rates than you would if your money was sitting in a savings account.

Your Stuff NeighborGoods.com allows you to lend people your stuff. If you have specialized things like ladders or tools that you don't use all the time, this is a great way to make a little extra money.

HOW TO PRICE YOUR GOODS
AND DETERMINE WHAT TO SELL

A quick online search is the easiest way to find out the going rate for any particular product. Once you have a target price range, you need to make sure it is worth your time to sell that product. First, add up all your costs. Then, calculate the time you have to spend making or handling that product to ensure that the price you can get for it compensates you appropriately for your time. Take into account if selling that product in bulk will reduce your costs or the time involved, and estimate how many products you'll be able to sell. If you're comfortable with the return on your investment and time that the product will give you, then sell the product for a similar price. If not, then find a product that will be more profitable.

MAKE MONEY ONLINE

It's easy to make money selling stuff online. Who hasn't sold a piece of furniture on Craigslist? But what if you want to do it as your side hustle? Unless you're a hoarder, you probably don't have enough extra bookcases to provide you with a supplementary monthly income. So what are your options? Here are some great ways to make money online:

Sell Crafts on Etsy If you're crafty, Etsy (www.etsy.com) is the place to be. From tricked out iPhone cases to handmade jewelry and vintage clothing, you can find almost anything on Etsy. Before you invest too much money setting up your Etsy empire, make sure there's a market for your goods. Make a variety of things and see what sells. Be sure to promote your wares on Pinterest and Instagram.

Design T-Shirts and Other Products Websites like Zazzle.com and Cafepress.com let you design products like T-shirts, stickers, bags, water bottles, Keds, and skateboard decks. The best thing about these sites is that you don't have to produce or ship the items. You just design them and the sites handle everything else. Finding a niche and promoting it with a website or blog definitely helps.

FIND A GOOD NICHE

There is a saying that goes "the riches are in the niches." When you're looking for a side hustle, consider drilling down into a niche. Very specific niches are often called long-tail niches. The long tail is the part of the market that doesn't usually get served by mainstream businesses because the market in the long tail isn't big enough for them. If you think, for example, about business books, there will typically be a larger group of people willing to purchase a general business book than a book about women launching startups. While there will still be a market for a book about women launching startups, a big publishing house might not be willing to invest the time and money to reach that market. With your side hustle, you can target those more limited long-tail markets and have few competitors.

Self-Publish There is a fairly robust market online for self-published genre fiction and very specific nonfiction. If you like writing romance, sci-fi, or erotica, you might find a fan base. If you have something to share about a very specific topic that would appeal to a large group of people, a nonfiction e-book could be a great side-hustle opportunity. You can easily sell e-books these days on websites like Amazon.com, BarnesandNoble.com, and Kobo.com.

Sell on Amazon People make a great side income selling products on Amazon. You can buy products wholesale from the United States or from overseas and list them on Amazon for sale.

Sell on eBay eBay.com is also a great way to sell things online. eBay tends to focus on used goods and specialty items. If you can find expensive jeans at a thrift store, you can often sell them for much more on eBay.

Start a Blog If you start a blog in a profitable niche, you can make money blogging. You can sign up for affiliate programs, display AdSense ads, and sell an e-book. While some people make absurd amounts of money blogging, still others make nothing. If you're trying to blog for money, learn everything you can from people who are successful at it.

SELL THINGS OFFLINE

There are far too many potential side hustles to list them all. In fact, some opportunities to make extra cash are right in your own backyard. Consider the following opportunities:

Farmers' Markets If you like to grow or make things, farmers' markets might be the place for you. People love artisanal food items and are willing to pay a premium for things that are local and homemade. To get set up, check out the food-handling requirements of your state and local farmers' markets and get all the certifications necessary to start your business.

Craft Fairs It seems like everywhere you look there are craft fairs populated by hip and trendy young crafters. If you make crafts, consider these fairs.

Flea Markets Flea markets are great places to sell things like clothing, electronics, books, jewelry, auto parts, and tools. Find things cheaply at estate sales, garage sales, and rummage sales, then sell them at your stall.

GET WORK ONLINE

TaskRabbit.com allows you to do small jobs and tasks like running errands or helping people move.

Zaarly.com allows you to market your services to other people. Currently, people offer everything from baking pies to repairing iPhones.

oDesk.com allows you to take on virtual-assistant jobs and get paid based on an hourly rate. While some jobs are long-term, others look for help in shorter stints.

Fiverr.com allows you to do small tasks for $5 each. You just need to find something that will appeal to a broad group and not take too much of your time.

FIND SIDE HUSTLE IDEAS AND TIPS

SmartPassiveIncome.com Considered an expert in the side-hustling field, Pat Flynn helps you find ways to make money online while you're doing other things.

BudgetsAreSexy.com This funny and informative blog has more than 50 side-hustle ideas and case studies.

MyWifeQuitHerJob.com Steve Chou talks about online business and how to successfully turn your side hustle into a full-time job.

PROVIDE SERVICES

Consider doing freelance work or consulting part-time. Before you start, however, make sure that your employer is okay with it. You don't want to lose your job because you tried making a few extra bucks. Here are a few ideas for service-related side hustles:

Focus on Seniors Seniors have a lot of needs that you can help fulfill. You can start a business driving seniors around on the weekends to do errands or helping them learn how to use computers.

Teach Your Skill If you have a skill that other people might want to learn, become a tutor or teach a workshop. For example, if you have a degree in English, consider becoming a writing tutor or teaching SAT prep.

Do Things People Hate Not many people like washing their cars, cutting their lawns, shoveling their snow, or picking up after their dogs. By focusing your side hustle on doing something that people don't like to do or are too busy to do, you can easily sell your service.

WHAT MAKES FOR A SUCCESSFUL SIDE HUSTLE?

If you want to know more about side hustles, Nick Loper is the person to ask. He is the chief side hustler at SideHustleNation.com and hosts the *Side Hustle Show* podcast, where he has new guests every week and explores different side hustles. Recently, he quit his day job to focus on his online businesses.

WHY DID HE SIDE HUSTLE? "I was looking to spend my free time more productively and generate income independent of a day job."

SIDE HUSTLE HIGHLIGHTS

The most profitable: Selling digital assets like books, courses, or software. Create something once and sell it as many times as you can.

The easiest to get into: Joining the "sharing economy" through services like Lyft, Uber, Airbnb, Postmates, TaskRabbit, and other similar things.

The most flexible: Freelancing. Sell some service or skill you excel at to businesses that need your help.

HOW DID HE BALANCE HIS SIDE HUSTLE WITH ENJOYING LIFE? "Enjoy your work; it's fun, challenging, and rewarding! Some colleagues have found success in scheduling dedicated time on their calendars or setting their alarms 30 to 60 minutes earlier in the morning."

HOW DID HE TURN HIS SIDE HUSTLE INTO HIS MAIN GIG? "Set a monthly income target and work toward that. You might even say, 'I want to earn $4,000 a month on average for six months before I give my notice.' It's a perfect bridge between a day job and becoming a full-time entrepreneur because it removes so much risk from the equation."

HACKS

VOLUNTEER

Candy Ho of *Career Connections Consulting* told me that joining the Board of Directors of a local charity helped her move her career forward because she was able to learn more about how to run an organization. She also suggested volunteering to be on committees at work: "By joining task forces and working committees, you're working with people outside your department, which will help you build your personal brand across the company and potentially open you up to new opportunities."

STOP WORRYING AND START LOVING YOUR JOB

Many people seem to believe that if they've chosen to do one thing right now they have therefore closed all other doors. That's not true. Nowadays, most people have five to seven careers over the course of their lifetimes. Instead of worrying that you've closed a door, take advantage of the opportunity you have in your current role to learn everything you can. That knowledge and experience might just be the perfect stepping stone to the next stage of your career.

LEARN TO MANAGE UP

When we talk about managing, we often talk about a boss managing an employee, but one of the most important things is learning to manage up. Most bosses are incredibly busy and have a lot of different things on their plates. Managing up means making your boss's job easier by providing him or her with everything he or she needs to be successful—even if he or she hasn't thought about it or asked for it. Managing up can also help your boss overcome his or her weaknesses. For example, if a boss has a problem keeping track of details on projects, you can create a system for them. The end result is that you look like you're a problem solver, and your boss is able to be more successful and effective.

MANAGE EXPECTATIONS

Don't make any promises you're not 100% certain you can deliver on. If you don't do something you committed to do, your colleagues or your boss will be less likely to trust you the next time around. Whenever you commit to doing something, give yourself some extra time to complete it. You never know what might happen to prevent you from delivering something on time. If you deliver what you've promised ahead of schedule, people will think you're a superstar. If you deliver late, they might think you're incompetent. By managing what people expect from you, you will always be able to under-promise and over-deliver.

JOB-PROOF YOUR SOCIAL MEDIA

Don't let your social media accounts keep you from getting or keeping a job. According to a study on CareerBuilder, around 50% of hiring managers disqualified candidates who posted provocative or inappropriate photos, 24% found proof on social media that candidates lied on their resumes, and 48% were turned off by evidence of excessive drinking or drug use. To keep yourself from being one of those casualties, keep your accounts private, don't post bad things about current or former employers, and delete any posts that could be seen as inappropriate.

Once you get the job, make it a rule to either not accept friend requests from coworkers or to only allow them to see a limited version of your profile.

FOCUS ON GETTING BIGGER CONTRACTS

When asked why she's been so successful as a freelancer, Trina Isakson of *27 Shift* responded that she "learned early on that it takes the same amount of effort to get a $1,000 contract as a $30,000 contract, so I spend my time on the larger contracts." Because she focuses on getting bigger contracts, she only needs to close three to four deals a year and can spend more time working instead of looking for work. To keep her focus, she's willing to say no to smaller contracts. If it's hard to find large contracts in your line of work, consider selling monthly subscriptions that will entitle your clients to a certain amount of your time every month.

PRESENT AT CONFERENCES

Trina Isakson from *27 Shift* suggests that young people should consider presenting at conferences. As a freelancer she says, "I present annually at a conference in my field where I meet academics and practitioners. I get a lot of my work that way." Presenting at conferences is a way to establish yourself as an expert in a particular field. In fact, think about it as an hour-long infomercial on you.

DON'T LOSE YOURSELF IN YOUR JOB

Margaret Lobenstine, author of *The Renaissance Soul*, cautions Millennials not to identify too closely with their jobs. According to Margaret, when you identify so closely with your job, "your bosses become the parents of your identity and you want to impress them so you're on all day. But when you've been on all day, at the end of the day you're exhausted." By cultivating interests and passions outside of what you do for a living, you're better able to weather the stresses of your workplace since you don't see everything that happens at work as jeopardizing your main source of value and identity.

KNOW YOUR "WHY"

Sometimes when things are difficult, it can be hard to stay motivated. Nick Loper of Side Hustle Nation thinks it's important to find your "why." According to Nick, "Sometimes the side-hustle path can be long and lonely, especially if you're chasing more 'passive income' strategies. If you have a clear picture of why you want to run your own business, and the customers you want to serve, you'll be more likely to press through the hard times." Nick's advice works for any situation. At some point in your career, you're going to get discouraged; being clear on why you're working so hard will make it easier to cope and overcome any difficulties.

SOLVE A REAL PAIN

Martin Zwilling from *Startup Professionals* suggests that the best way to build a successful business is to solve a problem that is painful enough to consumers or businesses that they are willing to pay for its solution. While it might seem simple, he sees far too many Millennial entrepreneurs trying to develop technology or create products that aren't necessary but are instead what he calls "nice-to-have." Says Zwilling, "If you can solve a real problem aimed at real customers who have real money, then you have the potential for making a real business. People don't buy things that are nice-to-have; they buy solutions to problems."

TREAD CAREFULLY AROUND REQUEST FOR PROPOSALS (RFPs)

Many freelancers get work by responding to RFPs, but Trina Isakson from *27 Shift* suggests you be choosy about which jobs you submit proposals to. One of the biggest problems with RFPs is that they take a lot of time to put together. Another problem is that they require you to give away a lot of advice and suggestions that you would typically charge clients for. Says Trina, "I don't give away my intellectual property for free."

LOOK AT CUTE ANIMALS

While it seems counterintuitive to suggest that looking at cute animal videos on YouTube will make you more productive, it turns out that science disagrees. Japanese researcher Hiroshi Nittono conducted an experiment that found that looking at pictures and videos of cute animals improves your mood at work and increases your productivity. The results showed that study participants were able to perform tasks that required focused attention better after viewing cute images. This is because baby faces induce care-giving impulses in the viewer and those impulses can help increase focus and concentration.

START WITH THE HARDEST THING

Opinions vary about whether you should start each day with a few easy tasks to ease yourself into the workday and build your confidence or do the hardest thing first. That said, by starting with something difficult, you won't feel like it's looming over you all day and you'll get a bigger confidence boost in the morning. Also, as the day goes by, your willpower gets used up and you're more likely to put it off another day if you wait to do it.

BREAK YOUR DAY INTO PRODUCTIVE CHUNKS

This will probably surprise no one, but it's unnatural to work a seven-to-eight-hour day nonstop without breaks and maintain a high level of productivity. As a species, humans are just not designed for that. It turns out that the longest period of time that we can concentrate on one thing intently is 90 minutes. After that, you're supposed to take a 15- to 20-minute break as your energy levels will start to lag. This 90-minute cycle is connected to a rhythm in our bodies called ultradian rhythm.

STOP MULTITASKING AND START BATCH PROCESSING

According to freelancer Nik Parks from *Launching Creative*, "When you work on a project for a client, respond to an email, grab a snack, watch a YouTube video, check your email again, work on a different project for a different client, and invoice an older client, it's a lot like driving in fog. Sure, you're going somewhere, but you aren't going in a clear direction and you're moving slowly." Nik suggests that you adopt a batch-processing method where you focus on one type of task at a time: "If you're going to focus on emails, do nothing but email for an established period of time."

BLOCK OR LIMIT YOUR INTERNET USAGE

Sometimes it can be difficult to get things done with Facebook, Twitter, Instagram, and all your favorite blogs singing their siren songs and leading you toward hours of procrastination. When you really need to get work done, consider using an app like Self-Control or Freedom to block your access to the Internet. If you find yourself wasting too much time on Instagram, an app like Anti-Social blocks your access to social media sites. If you don't think blocking yourself is a good idea, you can always install apps like Klok, RescueTime, Slife, and ManicTime. They work by giving you a readout of how you've used your time during the day so that you can see how much you've wasted and change your bad habits.

MAXIMIZE YOUR PRODUCTIVITY USING THE 80/20 RULE

Did you know that, on average, 80% of any person's outcomes come from just 20% of his or her output? Think about what you do at your job every day. What is the most important or productive part of your job? By that, I mean what do you do that provides the highest return for your company? If you're a salesperson that might be meeting or pitching high-value clients. You might spend 80% of your time pitching smaller clients or doing office work, but the majority of the sales you bring in might come from those high-value clients. Once you understand that 80% of your work is spent doing things that don't return a great deal of value, your goal should be to minimize the time you spend on these activities and maximize the time you spend on things that will yield desirable results.

PART

SPENDING IT

5

CHAPTER

PLANNING

Trying to retire comfortably without a financial plan is like trying to drive in an unfamiliar city without a map. You might eventually end up at your destination, but you're probably going to arrive late and having wasted a lot of gas. This chapter will explore the reasons that make knowing where you're at and where you're going so important.

YOU MIGHT BE BROKE, BUT YOU STILL NEED A PLAN

Not having a financial plan is normal. When you're in your twenties, you tend to be as busy as you are poor. You get depressed just looking at your bank statements and student loan bills. You wonder if you'll ever get to a point where you'll feel financially secure. You probably don't think about retirement because you have other worries.

But having financial plans is important for Millennials in both their twenties and their thirties. Living requires money, and you want to be able to retire comfortably. Money is one of the most important things in your life, but many people try to get by without a firm plan. Some might feel like it doesn't matter since they're not currently making enough money. Others feel like it's too complicated, confusing, or expensive to create a plan.

It's not as confusing, complicated, or expensive as you think. After all, a financial plan is just a roadmap for your financial life. It takes into account all the important things that you want to do in your life, helps you see what is possible, provides you with goals, and gives you options and ideas for the future (See Figure 4).

DIY FINANCIAL PLANNING

Most people think that you have to go to a financial advisor or a financial planner to create a financial plan. While working with a professional can make the task easier, you can also create your own financial plan. If you choose to DIY, here are the steps you'll need to take.

Determine Your Current Net Worth This might be a depressing exercise if you have student loans or other large amounts of debt; you might owe more money than you have. Knowing your current net worth gives you an idea of where you're starting from. To determine your net worth, add up the value of all your assets (if you have them) and subtract

FIGURE 4

THE FINANCIAL PLANNING PROCESS

Here's what good financial planning looks like:

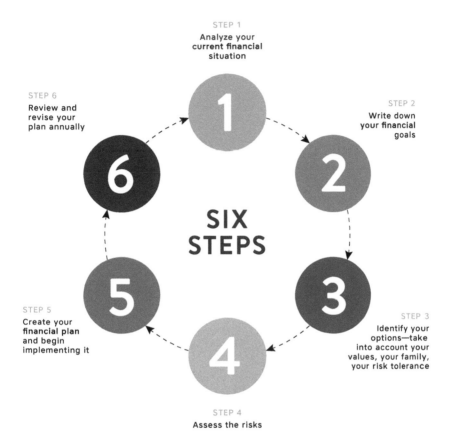

STEP 1
Analyze your
current financial
situation

STEP 2
Write down
your financial
goals

STEP 3
Identify your
options—take
into account your
values, your family,
your risk tolerance

STEP 4
Assess the risks

STEP 5
Create your
financial plan
and begin
implementing it

STEP 6
Review and
revise your
plan annually

SIX STEPS

the value of any debts you owe. If the number you get at the end of it makes you cringe, don't worry. Creating a financial plan is the first step to ensuring you can feel great about that number in a few years.

List Your Goals The first thing you need to do is start with the bigger picture and figure out what your short- and long-term financial goals are. Do you want to own a home, have children, travel the world, or retire early? Do you want to pay off debt, save money for a down payment, go on a trip, or buy a new car in the near future? Make a list of all the financial goals you have for your life. Feel free to list anything you might want to do someday, even if it seems extravagant or impossible. Once you have a list of all your goals, you can prioritize them.

Give Your Goals $ Figures Once you have your goals ranked, you'll need to determine how much each goal will cost you. Short-term goals will be easier to estimate cost for. You can easily look up how much a trip or a new car will cost you. It will be harder to determine the cost of having children or retiring comfortably. Retiring comfortably means different things for different people.

Develop a Budget Budgets allow you to decide what you should allocate to current spending and what you should allocate to your savings goals. We'll cover budgeting in the next chapter. For advice on how to prioritize saving versus debt repayment, see Chapter 14.

Develop a Debt-Repayment Plan A debt-repayment plan will include a forecast of how much you intend to pay each month toward your debt and how long it will take you to pay it off. It will also include a strategy describing how you will prioritize which debt to pay off first.

Create an Investment Plan Once you have some long-term savings, it helps to work out an investment plan. There are a number of different assets to consider and a number of different ways to invest. From a 401(k) to a Roth IRA to 529 plans to unsheltered investment accounts, you will need to decide where your money is going to make the most impact. Each type of account has different criteria and was designed to fill a different need, explained in greater detail in Chapter 15.

THE DIFFERENCE BETWEEN A FINANCIAL PLANNER AND A FINANCIAL ADVISOR

When you're looking for financial advice, be sure to go to the proper source for it. In the financial services industry, you'll run into financial advisors and financial planners. A financial or investment advisor can help you invest your money, but they often work on commission and are charged with selling you particular financial products. Certified Financial Planners (CFP) are advisors who work primarily in their clients' best interest and provide comprehensive financial planning advice. CFPs can help you with anything from investment planning to taxes and estate plans.

Create a Tax Plan As you plan, it's important to factor tax consider-ations into your decisions. For example, you can deduct the interest of things like mortgages and student loans from your taxes. That reduces the loan's overall cost. Familiarize yourself with those deductions you qualify for in order to maximize your tax savings.

Create Savings or Spending Challenges Once your financial plan is completed, you might notice the need to make changes in your spending to meet your goals. Come up with some strategies to help you make more and spend less. Create quarterly and annual challenges and work toward them.

Update It Congratulations, you've made a comprehensive financial plan! Now you can sit back and coast until you retire, right? Not so fast! You need to do an annual check-in to ensure that you're on track and to make any necessary tweaks. Table 6 looks at a few apps that can help you manage your financial planning.

FEELING OVERWHELMED?

Financial planning can seem like a lot of work, and it can feel overwhelming. A 2013 study by Nationwide Funds found that 26% of investors didn't have a financial plan. Also, some people create financial plans, but then have a hard time sticking to them. If you're concerned about your ability to create and stick to a financial plan, here are some tips to make it easier.

TABLE 6

APPS TO HELP WITH FINANCIAL PLANNING

THE APP	WHAT IT DOES
The Pocket Financial Planner	Lets you compare yourself to well-known financial benchmarks to show you how well you're doing. It helps you realize where you have some work to do and what to prioritize.
Forbes Lifetime Financial Planning	Allows you to test different scenarios, such as getting a new job or having children, to see how they will affect your financial situation to help you plan for your financial future.
Personal Capital	Analyzes your income, spending, and investments in order to show you how a few tweaks can help you significantly along the way.
LearnVest	Helps you plan for everyday purchases and major life events like getting married. Track your spending, set goals, and work toward them with LearnVest's app.

PEOPLE AREN'T STICKING TO THEIR FINANCIAL PLANS

According to the "Stick With It" report, while 77% of Americans set financial goals, only 55% claim to be self-disciplined in their financial lives. There are lots of reasons why it can be difficult to stick to a financial plan. In fact, Northwestern Mutual[5] commissioned a report studying Americans attitudes toward their financial lives, which found that 63% thought the fast pace of today's world made it more difficult to stick to long-term goals. If you do take the time to create a financial plan, do your best to stick to it. Your plan can only work if you put it into effect.

Get a Professional Creating a financial plan for yourself might be on your to-do list, but if you never seem to get around to actually creating it, then you should consider going to a professional. Choose a fee-based financial planner to help you—one who doesn't receive a commission for any products recommended. While this may be expensive, it's an important investment in your financial future.

Check In More Often If you're having a hard time sticking to your financial plan, you might consider trying to check in on your plan more frequently. Set up a monthly or quarterly appointment with yourself to sit down and evaluate your financial goals and what you've done to achieve them. By reminding yourself of your goals, they will be at the top of your mind the next time you're tempted to deviate from your financial plan. Also, know you're not alone.

Make Financial Planning Fun Financial planning doesn't have to be a boring, solitary process. In fact, experts suggest that those who share their financial goals with friends are more likely to reach them. Get your friends together or a group of couples together to help motivate one another to create and stick to financial plans. Make the meetings fun by challenging one another to create frugal appetizers or treats to share.

WHAT MILLENNIALS NEED TO KNOW ABOUT FINANCIAL PLANNING

If you're looking for an expert on financial planning for Millennials, look no further than Sophia Bera, the founder of *Gen Y Planning*. She delivers comprehensive financial planning to Millennials across the country via video calls—and she knows everything you need to know about planning.

ON WHY MILLENNIALS NEED FINANCIAL PLANNERS "Millennials are asking some great questions when it comes to money, although they don't realize these are financial-planning questions. For example, they're asking things like 'Should I buy or should I rent?' and 'Should I save in a Roth IRA or a 401(k)?' A financial planner helps answer those questions."

ON WHY ONLY FEW MILLENNIALS HAVE FINANCIAL PLANNERS "Financial planning typically was expensive. Many financial planners charge on assets under management, and they have minimums, which means you might have to have $250,000 to $1 million in your investment accounts in order for a financial planner to even work with you. They would then charge around 1% a year in order to manage these financial assets. Since most Millennials don't have that much money in their investment accounts, we need to change the way we are charging. I charge my clients an initial planning fee and then by a monthly subscription fee, just like they would pay for their gym memberships or cell phone bills."

ON HOW FINANCIAL PLANNING FOR MILLENNIALS IS DIFFERENT "The problem with many financial-planning firms is that when they try to attract Millennials, they just send the same sixty-year-old white guy to the initial meeting and just give the Happy Meal version of a financial plan. We have to completely rethink the way we do financial planning with Millennials and actually address their needs and concerns in a different way.

In addition to traditional financial-planning categories, I believe there are a number of other areas that make up a financial plan for Millennials. Oftentimes, my clients have student loans so I help them figure out their plan to pay off the student loans. I talk to my clients about things like credit and rewards, and help them get the most out of their credit cards. Millennials are also more interested in achieving financial independence rather than working toward their retirement."

ON THE POINT AT WHICH YOU SHOULD HIRE A FINANCIAL PLANNER "If you have a ton of credit card debt, get out of credit card debt first. As your financial situation becomes more complex—and you don't really have the time to tend to it—then you should look at hiring a financial planner. A lot of times that happens when people are in their late 20s and early 30s; their financial situations become more complicated. They might've just gotten married or just bought a home."

HOW ARE FINANCIAL PLANNERS USING TECHNOLOGY TO TARGET MILLENNIALS? "Financial planners working with Millennials have an opportunity to use technology more than we have in the past. I do video calls with most of my clients. Though I have a few local clients who I will meet in person, I mostly work virtually. I think that there are a lot more Millennials who are looking for a financial planner who can meet them when they're available. They don't want to take half a day off of work, schedule a two hour meeting and drive downtown to meet you with a shoebox of financial documents.

Instead, technology allows us to streamline those things like gathering the documents in advance electronically. I also send my clients electronic bills and contracts. All these things are new for the profession that I'm in. Financial planners are just starting to work virtually with our clients. In the future, I think we'll see more of client portals where both you and the client can see all the financial information at the same time and then you can work together while viewing the same information. That would provide the opportunity for more proactive financial planning rather than reactive planning."

CHAPTER

BUDGETING

When you're planning to go on a road trip, do you get into the driver's seat and put on a blindfold? Probably not. When you spend without a budget, you're basically driving blind. If you've never created a budget before, you need to start by analyzing where you're spending your money. This chapter will help you create a budget—and stick to it.

THREE ESSENTIAL THINGS TO CONSIDER WHEN CREATING A BUDGET

1. If You're the Couple That Budgets Together Who doesn't love talking money with their significant other? Anyone? It's important that you do anyway. Some couples find that household budgets allow them to live more effectively together and plan for the future; still, other couples think household budgets are the worst that could happen to their relationship. Often what separates one type of couple from the other is how closely their values around money and savings are aligned.

If one is a saver and the other is a spender, you might find that budgeting styles clash. The spenders might feel like the savers are trying to control them, while the savers might feel frustrated that the spenders aren't taking as much responsibility as they are. It's not a deal breaker to have different financial values and styles, but it means that you'll both need to compromise.

2. Do You Need a Category for Green Running Shoes? Once you have a clear idea of where you're spending your money, categorize your spending. For example, some people track how much they spend at the grocery store, at restaurants, and at cafes separately. This can be incredibly helpful if they want to challenge themselves to cut back in one of these areas.

Other people like to track all these items under the heading of "Food," giving them more flexibility in how they spend their money. Similarly, some people like to make separate categories to cover "Shopping" and track things like spending on books, clothes, or items for their kids. Specific categories can also be useful to track changes in spending over time in certain categories.

3. To Rollover or Not to Rollover Let's say you've budgeted to spend $100 per month on gas. If you spend $75 on gas one month, do you plan to have the other $25 rollover to the next month? Some people choose not to allow their budget to rollover so that they can trick themselves into saving that money.

THINGS THAT PEOPLE FORGET TO BUDGET FOR

If you don't budget for infrequent or unexpected expenses, you might have a hard time fitting them into your budget when they crop up. Many people forget to budget for things like gifts, for example. People also often forget to budget for seasonal expenses like gardening supplies and new seasonal clothing or shoes, or infrequent expenses like property taxes and car maintenance. If you pay your insurance on a yearly basis, make sure you put some money aside each month so that it will be there when you need it. Don't forget to budget for contributions to an emergency fund or to a vacation fund. Other things that people forget to budget for are charitable contributions, parking, household maintenance, haircuts, and medical copays.

Others like having budget categories rollover so that they can find a balance in their spending over time. For example, if you were too busy to go out for dinner one month, it might be nice to have a little more money the next month to treat yourself. See Table 7 for guidelines on how much to save.

FEAST OR FAMINE: WHAT TO DO IF YOU UNDERSPEND OR OVERSPEND

If you're constantly underspending in particular categories, consider adjusting your budget and either allocating that money to another expense or allocating it to savings. If you're overspending in particular categories, adjust accordingly. If you're always overspending on your entire budget, try to take measures to reduce your spending (for example, by moving to a cheaper apartment) or increase your income with a side hustle or second job.

TABLE 7

HOW MUCH SHOULD YOU BUDGET?

Financial experts disagree on the specifics of how much you should spend on different categories since, depending on where you live, you might need to allocate more money to a particular category than another. Here are my suggestions for allocating after-tax income:

CATEGORY	HOW MUCH OF YOUR MONTHLY INCOME YOU SHOULD SPEND
Total Housing Costs	20% to 30%
Transportation	5% to 15%
Food	7% to 12%
Loan Repayment	5% to 15%
Personal Expenses	5% to 12%
Health Care	12% to 20%
Utilities	4% to 7%
Savings	10% to 25%
Entertainment	1% to 5%

STRATEGIES TO HELP YOU STICK TO YOUR BUDGET

Now that you've spent all this time creating a budget, how do you make sure you stick to it? Here are a few strategies.

Know Why You're Doing It You decided to make a budget for an important reason. Maybe you were gradually sinking further into credit card debt every month and you wanted to regain control. Perhaps you're saving up for an important life event like getting married or having a child. Whatever the reason, try to remember it whenever you're tempted to overspend.

Don't Make Dramatic Changes If you've always splurged on an afternoon coffee and you suddenly declare that you're never buying coffee again, you're going to fail. Developing new habits takes time. You're much more likely to succeed if you gradually make changes in how you spend money.

Keep Your Pleasures Don't cut all the fun out of your life. Keep a few things in your budget for you. Decide what will give you the most bang for your buck and keep that in your budget. If you're having trouble making choices, try using the following worksheet to wrap your head around monthly numbers.

Give Yourself Rewards Find a way to reward yourself for your good behavior. Budgeting can make you weary after a while, especially if you deny yourself some of the things you used to enjoy. Your reward might not cost anything or it might be something cheap. You might also decide to allocate unspent money in a category toward your reward or budget some money for a reward. See Table 8 for some ideas of inexpensive alternatives to past splurges.

Pay Yourself First If you have a hard time sticking to your budget, consider having the money allocated for your savings automatically moved into your savings account and out of your greedy little hands.

Do It Intermittently If you can't stick to the process of tracking your budget on a long-term basis, consider tracking your spending for one month every quarter. That way you aren't locked into the process of budgeting all the time, but you intermittently get a reality check on your finances that potentially encourages you to spend less and save more. While this isn't ideal, it's much better than nothing and will likely help you develop better habits.

TABLE 8

BUDGET-FRIENDLY ALTERNATIVES

Feeling like you're depriving yourself can lead you to act out and blow your budget. Rather than denying yourself something, find an alternative that is cheaper but just as fun.

INSTEAD OF THIS	DO THIS
Buying new clothes	Buy accessories—a new necklace or a new tie will help update your look and will fit in your budget
Going out with friends	Invite them over—making dinner or hosting a potluck will be much cheaper, especially if you make it BYOB
Buying magazines and books	Trade or get them from the library—swapping magazines and books with friends will save you money
Cable	Netflix or Amazon Prime—they are cheaper than cable, and you still get great content
Brand names	Buy generic—you'll get the same product for a fraction of the price

WHAT CAN BUDGETS DO FOR YOU?

J. Money is the author of the popular blog *Budgets Are Sexy*. He's not your average personal finance blogger. When he bought a $350,000 house on a whim in 2007, he had to get serious about his finances. Here, he shares his hard-earned wisdom with you.

ON WHY BUDGETS ARE SEXY "Budgets are sexy because they give you confidence. Confidence in knowing where your money's going every month, confidence in being able to make quick decisions on the fly, and confidence in your financial future."

ON THE MOST IMPORTANT STEPS TO TAKE TO SET UP A BUDGET "The most important thing to figure out is what it costs you to live on a monthly basis. Once you know what you spend every month, compare it to your total take home pay and see what the difference is. This is the second most important number to know, and it's a sobering one. This gap tells you roughly how much you have leftover every month to help accomplish your goals. And if it's less than desired, it's time to make some changes!"

ON WHAT PEOPLE DO WRONG WHEN BUDGETING "Expecting different results by doing the exact same things every day. Tracking your money alone won't change the future; you actually have to change your habits to affect it. Budgeting itself isn't that complicated at all (spend less than you make), but the lifestyles we live are. Do whatever it takes to keep your goals front and center, and all the small changes will eventually get you there!"

ON WHAT HE LEARNED FROM BUDGETING "Once you get good at it, you actually don't have to pay attention to it as much anymore! It sounds contrary to everything I just stated, but budgeting is as much a habit as learning how to swim or ride a bike. Once you know what you're doing, you don't have to keep the training wheels on at all times."

MONTHLY BUDGET WORKSHEET

INCOME

PARTNER 1

Monthly Take-home
Pay from Main Job...... ....

Monthly Take-home
from Side Hustles....... ....

Other Income ....

PARTNER 2

Monthly Take-home
from Main Job ....

Monthly Take-home
from Side Hustles ....

Other Income ....

Total Income .... [   ]

EXPENSES

HOUSING AND UTILITIES

Mortgage or Rent....... ....

Home or Tenant
Insurance ....

Electricity.................... ....

Water............................ ....

Gas ....

Cable ....

Cell Phone ....

Home Phone............... ....

Internet....................... ....

Property Tax................ ....

Maintenance............... ....

Renovation Fund........ ....

Gardening................... ....

CAR

Car Payment ....

Car Insurance ....

Parking........................ ....

Gas ....

AAA Membership........ ....

Maintenance ....

License......................... ....

OTHER TRANSPORTATION

Transit ....

Car Share.................... ....

Taxi............................... ....

Bike Expenses ....

FOOD

Groceries ....

Restaurants................. ....

Coffee ....

Alcohol......................... ....

ENTERTAINMENT AND FITNESS

Gym Membership........ ....

Sports........................... ....

Entertainment ....

Hobbies........................ ....

Club............................... ....

TAXES AND DEBT REPAYMENT

Student Loan Debt .....

Credit Card Debt ....

Line of Credit ....

Taxes ....

Annual Credit Card Fees ....

Bank Charges ....

SHOPPING

Personal Items ....

Beauty ....

Clothes ....

Computer ....

Cell Phone ....

Other Items ....

PET

Pet Food ....

Pet Insurance ....

Vet Bills ....

Medication ....

Pet Toys and Treats ....

GIFTS

Gifts for Family ....

Gifts for Friends ....

Wedding Gifts ....

Holiday Gifts ....

CHILDREN

Childcare ....

Children's Clothing .....

Personal Items ....

Toys ....

SAVINGS

Emergency Fund ....

Savings Account ....

Down Payment Fund ....

401K ....

IRA ....

MEDICAL

Life Insurance ....

Health Insurance ....

Health Savings Account ....

Copays and Deductibles ....

Dental ....

Drugs ....

Glasses/Contacts ....

OTHER

Charity ....

Vacation ....

Course Fees ....

Course Books ....

Child Support ....

Alimony ....

Dry Cleaning ....

App Purchases ....

Can't Say No Fund .....

Other Expenses ....

Total Expenses ....

Total Income ....

Total Expenses ....   −

Monthly Balance ....   =

7

SHOPPING

The fundamentals of smart shopping are always the same: you have a budget, and it's your job to figure out how to get the most for it. As anyone's trip to the shops can attest, shopping can be delightful. Still, we all need to find a balance between what we want and what we need. This chapter will help you do so.

THE SHOPPING COMMANDMENTS

If there were such things as savings gods, they would probably provide us with "The Shopping Commandments" to keep our shopping under control. Since they don't exist, here are some general rules—rules that will save you thousands of dollars over your lifetime.

1. Thou Shalt Not Cheap Out Many personal finance writers will tell you how to find deals, but if you're planning on using something for a long time, you're much better off spending a little more and buying something that's of superior quality. Buying something with a lifetime warrantee can mean buying something once instead of buying the same product over and over each time it breaks. Some brands offer lifetime warranties on their products, including Jansport, Zippo, REI, Sierra Trading Post, Oxo utensils, Bogs Footwear, All Clad, Pampered Chef Cookwear, Davek Umbrellas, Tupperware, Craftsman Tools, Coach, Land's End, L.L. Bean, Otterbox, The North Face, Vermont Teddy Bears, Briggs and Riley Luggage, Swiftwick Socks, Polar Bottles, and many others.

Even if you're not buying a product with a lifetime warranty, you're still often better off buying something that will last for years than buying something that you'll need to replace in six months. You might save money in the short term by buying a cheaper solution, but you'll pay more over time.

2. Thou Shalt Love Dollar Stores While this commandment might seem to contradict the first one, there are some things that you really ought to be buying at a dollar store. Dollar stores can provide you with amazing savings on products that are identical to ones that cost more elsewhere. While there are certain things like garbage bags and cotton swabs that you should avoid buying at dollar stores because the quality isn't very good, you can get great deals on office supplies, gift wrap and party supplies, craft supplies, snacks, and kitchen items. Still, extreme deals have their limits.

DON'T BECOME A COUPON-CHASER

We've all seen the extreme couponing shows. There's something about seeing someone get hundreds of dollars of food for only a few cents that appeals to us on a primal level. But if you watch enough of those shows, you'll see that the coupon-chasers devote hours upon hours to those successful shopping trips. Some dumpster-dive for old newspapers, others spend hours clipping coupons with their kids, all of them scrutinize store flyers, and most have obsessively organized coupon binders. That's a full-time job. And what do they get at the end of it? Processed food that isn't even that good for them or their families and brands that they might not even like. If they spent that time working a part-time job or freelancing from home, they would be able to afford what they want.

3. *Thou Shalt Not Be Fooled* If you buy something on a regular basis, consider doing an occasional audit to see if you're actually saving money. For example, many people believe that if they buy in bulk, they'll save overall. While sometimes you save money by buying in large quantities, there are certain products that you actually might end up paying more for. Stores like Costco and Sam's Club offer some great deals on packaged foods and meats but often don't provide the same level of savings on things like paper towels or fresh produce. If you're spending a significant amount of money on something, you should be checking to make sure you're actually getting a deal. See Tables 9 and 10 for tips on how to save and what items to stop wasting money on.

4. *Thou Shalt Ditch Your Brand Loyalty* People can get very passionate about the brands that they love. At the end of the day, your loyalty should be to your pocketbook and not to a company that sees you as a dollar figure. Sure, the people at one company might use cute cats to market their products, but that doesn't make their products better. There's nothing wrong with trying out an off-label brand.

TABLE 9
THINGS YOU SHOULD STOP WASTING MONEY ON

WHAT	WHY
Expensive face creams & moisturizers	There is no difference between expensive and cheap ones.
In-app purchases	They add up!
Spice mixes	You can easily mix your own.
Coffee creamers	They're filled with chemicals and are easy to substitute.
Bottled water	Buy a bottle and fill it with water.
Body wash	Soap is much cheaper.
Paper towels	Use tea towels and cloth napkins instead.
ATM fees	Get a no-fee checking account instead.
Lottery tickets	Your chances of winning are about the same as your chances of being declared President of the World.

5. Thou Shalt Stock Up When It's on Sale There are certain times of the year when you can expect things to go on sale. For example, if you want to stock up on condiments, do that in the summer, right before Independence Day when supermarkets are trying to lure you in with BBQ promotions. Similarly, if you love wearing perfume or cologne, you're going to get the best deals right before and right after the holiday season. While seasonal sales are great, there are also sales that happen at regular intervals of four to six weeks. Stock your shelves when the prices are cheap. See Tables 11 and 12 for tips on when to buy particular items.

6. Thou Shalt Outsmart the Sales Person If you're on the market for a more expensive item, be sure to do your research. Know how much you want to spend before you go into the store. Sales people are trained to try to get you to spend more money. Prices are created with the specific intent to get you to open up your wallet just a little wider to get what seems like a much better deal. Always try to set a budget before you go to the store to purchase anything. The last thing you need is to get in there and have the salesperson talk you into something you can't afford.

TABLE 10

HOW TO SAVE BIG MONEY

METHOD	ESTIMATED SAVINGS IN ONE YEAR
Bring Your Lunch to Work	$1,300
Renegotiate Your Phone and Cable Bills	$250 to $600
Practice Meatless Monday	$200 to $500
Ride Your Bike to Work	$2,600*
Grow Your Own Food	$500 to $1,000
Get a Better Rate on Car Insurance	$200 to $500

* Based on spending $50 in gas per week to commute to work

TABLE 11

BEST TIMES OF THE YEAR TO BUY CERTAIN ITEMS

According to *Consumer Reports*,[6] there are better times during the year to buy different items.

MONTH	WHAT TO BUY
January	Bedding, toys, workout equipment, winter clothing
February	Furniture, humidifiers, workout equipment
March	Digital cameras, TVs, small electronics, winter sports gear
April	Laptop computers, desktops computers, digital cameras, lawnmowers, spring clothing
May	Athletic gear, camping equipment, carpeting, cordless phones
June	Camcorders, pots, pans and dishware, carpeting, computers, swimwear
July	Outdoor furniture, swimwear, camcorders
August	Air conditioners, backpacks, dehumidifiers, outdoor furniture, snow blowers
September	Bikes, digital cameras, gas grills, plants, snow blowers
October	Winter coats, gas grills, computers, jeans
November	Baby products, bikes, GPS navigators, toys, TVs
December	Bikes, home appliances, TVs, toys, consumer electronics, camcorders

TABLE 12
WHEN FOOD IS IN SEASON

By buying certain foods when they're in season, you'll get them at their lowest prices. According to the USDA,[7] these are the best season deals:

SEASON	FRUIT
Winter	Grapefruit, kale, lemons, mushrooms, onions and leeks, oranges, pears, potatoes, sweet potatoes, turnips, winter squash
Spring	Apricots, broccoli, cabbage, green beans, honeydew melon, lettuce, mangos, mushrooms, onions and leeks, peas, pineapple, rhubarb, spinach, strawberries
Summer	Apricots, beets, bell peppers, blackberries, blueberries, cantaloupe, cherries, corn, cucumbers, eggplant, garlic, grapefruit, grapes, green beans, honeydew melon, kiwifruit, lima beans, mushrooms, peaches, peas, plums, radishes, raspberries, strawberries, summer squash, tomatoes, watermelon, zucchini
Fall	Apples, beets, broccoli, Brussels sprouts, carrots, cauliflower, cranberries, garlic, ginger, grapes, mushrooms, parsnips, pears, pineapple, pumpkins, sweet potatoes, winter squash

7. Thou Shalt Consider the Cost While we often will look at the price of something, we don't always think about the cost. By cost, I mean how much time you have to spend working in order to afford something. If you're lusting after a big screen TV, think about how long you will have to work in order to purchase it. Ask yourself if it is worth devoting that many hours of your life to buying it. If it is, great—enjoy your TV. If you decide it isn't, find a better use of that money.

ONLINE VS. HIGH STREET

Beyond making it easy to quickly compare prices between a number of different stores, shopping online can save you time and gas by not going to a physical store. You can usually find items cheaper online, and shopping online tends to reduce impulse buys. The downside of online shopping is that you sometimes have to pay for shipping or spend a minimum amount in order to qualify for free shipping.

BEST WEBSITES AND APPS FOR COMPARING PRODUCTS AND PRICES

Amazon.com With its rating systems and customer comments, Amazon has basically crowd-sourced consumer product testing.

Goodreads.com If you're wondering if you will like a book you're interested in reading, Goodreads can tell you if other people liked it and why.

ConsumerReports.org Consumer Reports tests products rigorously and gives you the details about what works and what doesn't.

Google Shopping No matter what you're looking for, Google Shopping will help you compare prices for the product across thousands of retailers.

Smoopa It's an app that lets you compare the price in store to prices online to ensure you're not overpaying.

Shopzilla.com With more than 100 million products listed, this site can help you find what you need at the price you want.

CALCULATE YOUR HAPPINESS RETURN ON INVESTMENT (ROI)

Lule Demmissie, managing director for TD Ameritrade, has a unique strategy for determining what you should buy with your hard-earned money. According to Lule, "Millennials hear too often that the money they spend on their daily Starbucks is bad or that they shouldn't be spending money on going out to restaurants or that they should be saving more. However, if spending money on those things makes you happy, prioritize them." Lule believes that you should cut expenses that give you the least amount of happiness, which will make sticking to your budget easier. Says Lule, "Money is no different than many elements of our lives; we need to respect how our behavior influences how we save it. If we don't, we may find ourselves crafting grand plans for savings only during New Year's resolutions and falling off shortly thereafter."

ARE THE SAVINGS WORTH IT?

Being frugal is important. But, if you're spending an hour doing something that will save you $10, consider if it would make more sense to take on a side hustle that will allow you to spend that hour earning $20. Your time is potentially worth money. By using all your free time trying to be frugal, you forget that there's a more productive way to spend your time.

BEST THINGS TO BUY ONLINE

Vitamins and Herbal Supplements You'll find better selections and cheaper prices on herbal supplements and vitamins online. Check out **iHerb.com**, **eVitamins.com**, and **Vitacost.com**.

Contact Lenses and Eyeglasses It's much easier to get your contacts and glasses online—and the price differences will surprise and delight you. Check out **Coastal.com**, **VisionDirect.com**, and **1800contacts.com**.

Specialty Foods Are you gluten-free? Do you follow the Paleo diet? If you do and can't find great products locally, consider searching online. Check out **Amazon.com**, **GlutenFreeDelivers.com**, and **WildMountainPaleo.com**.

Travel Sure, you can call a travel agent, but shopping online for travel can be much easier and cheaper. Check out **Kayak.com**, **Priceline.com**, and **Hipmunk.com**.

THINGS TO NEVER BUY ONLINE

Shopping online is convenient, but going into an actual store where you can see the product and potentially try it out can be better—especially if you need to get something quickly. Consider supporting local businesses since much more of the money you spend goes back into the local economy. You can also get great deals on shopping locally through sites like Groupon.com and Living Social.

Used High-End Designer Goods The chances are too high that you'll be buying counterfeit goods.

ARE YOU A SHOPAHOLIC?

Shopaholic might sound like a silly word, but having a hard time controlling shopping impulses isn't a laughing matter. Some people are addicted to shopping just like others are addicted to drugs, food, or alcohol. People with compulsive buying disorder (CBD) are often overcome by a strong urge to buy things when something bad happens or when they are under stress. They spend a lot of time shopping and often spend more money than they can afford to spend. For them, shopping provides temporary relief from their problems. Those with CBD often have mild to severe credit card debt because of their addiction and may hide their purchases from others. Luckily, cognitive-behavioral therapy has been shown to be an effective treatment.

Last-Minute Holiday Gifts Even if the website says that it will arrive before the holidays, don't take the chance. You can easily end up on the phone with customer service trying to track down your package during the peak of the holiday season. Not fun.

Anything Heavy The reason is pretty obvious—shipping fees will be through the roof for anything heavy!

RENTING VS. BUYING

Nowadays, sharing is considered the future of business. While people traditionally rented things like tuxedoes and carpet steamers, now you can rent almost anything, including cars, tools, bikes, and even luxury dresses. People love the idea of renting rather than buying, not only because it is often cheaper to do so, but also because many people want to live more simply.

One way to calculate whether you should rent or buy something is to calculate your cost per use. To do this, take the price of the product and subtract the amount you would be able to get for it if you sold it used at a later date. Be sure to factor in the space that storing the product will take up. If your price per use adds up to more than a rental fee would, then rent, don't buy.

YOU CAN NEGOTIATE THAT

Medical Bills Hospitals and doctors charge people who don't have insurance or who have minimal insurance far more than they charge people who do. That's because they've worked out deals with insurance companies to reduce their costs. If you ever get hit with an enormous medical bill, consider negotiating it down to a more manageable amount. Ask if they will let you pay the insurance or Medicare rate.

"BUY NOTHING" DAYS AND VOLUNTARY SIMPLICITY

In recent years, there has been a movement toward buying and spending less. Buy Nothing Day was started by artist Ted Dave and Adbusters to protest consumerism in 1994. In the United States, it takes place to coincide with Black Friday and it encourages participants to make a commitment to consuming less and producing less waste. The concept has caught on, however, among many personal finance writers—some of whom advocate days, weeks, or months where you commit to buying nothing or to only buying necessities. At the same time, a trend called voluntary simplicity, where people choose to give away most of their things and make a commitment to stop acquiring more, has begun to gain traction. Whether it's parents asking people to stop buying toys for their children or couples choosing to live in "tiny houses," the people of this movement promote the freedom it provides from financial stresses and the clutter of possessions.

Plumbing and Other Work If you want to get work done on your house, paying with cash can often get you a discount. Plumbers and other handymen will offer 20% or more off if you pay cash.

Rent Landlords hate having to find new tenants. It takes time out of their lives; they need to deal with the stress of potentially not having a tenant for a few months or getting bad tenants. If you've been a good tenant and your landlords like you, consider asking them for a break in your rent for staying around for another year.

Gym Memberships There is a lot of wiggle room on gym memberships, especially if you go at the end of the month when the staff members are trying to meet their sales targets. Tell the salesperson you're considering a competitor and you might get a deal.

Furniture If you like a particular couch but think it's too expensive, tell the salesperson. Most furniture stores are able to give you a discount if you buy multiple pieces from them or if they need to move products. It's particularly easy to negotiate a lower price for mattresses.

Floor or Display Models You can often get a discount on floor or display models. Tell them that you're interested in the floor model but that it's a bit above your budget and see what they can do for you.

Fees There are all sorts of fees that you can get waived or reduced. If you have to pay a fee, always ask if it can be waived. It won't hurt to ask, and you might just get what you want.

Cable and Phone Companies want you to pay more than you have to. They only really offer deals to new customers. But if you've been a loyal customer, call them up and ask if they will give you a deal. If you hint that you're thinking of switching your provider, they will be even more motivated to keep you happy.

NEW VS. USED

While there are some things you should really always buy new, others are usually perfectly good secondhand. Here is where to draw the line between the store and the yard sale.

THINGS TO ALWAYS BUY NEW

Shoes Shoes form to the feet of the first person who wears them and they can transfer fungi. Pass on buying used shoes.

Mattresses and Couches There are so many reasons why you don't want to buy a used mattress or couch. Stay away from used mattresses and couches.

Car Seats Babies and toddlers make a mess out of car seats. Often, the padding can't be washed and is harboring all sorts of bacteria. Avoid used car seats.

Cribs Babies die every year from unsafe cribs. You don't want it to happen to you. You're much better off getting a new crib that you know is sturdy.

THINGS TO ALWAYS BUY USED

Work Clothes and Jeans You can find high-end and designer clothing for pennies on the dollar at thrift stores and consignment shops. Depending on how often you buy clothes, buying used can really help you save.

Wedding Dresses It might seem less romantic to buy a used wedding gown, but if you use the money you save to go on an amazing honeymoon, it will all be worth it.

Kitchen Items You can get great prices on used dishes, utensils, baking implements, and glasses.

Office Furniture If you live in a city with small apartments, you might have even better luck and get it free. People who are moving to places that don't have room for their desks will be desperate to unload them.

Jewelry You can buy used jewelry for a fraction of the price of new jewelry—just make sure that it's real.

Video Games Why pay full price when you can wait a week for someone to beat the game and put it up for sale online?

Bikes Why pay full price for an expensive bike when you can get a great ride for a fraction of the cost? You can find great deals on sites like Craigslist or at police auctions.

Tools Many people buy tools they never use. Be one of the people to benefit from this—not one of the people sheepishly selling that drill they haven't used in two years.

FIGURE 5

HOW MANY SHIRTS CAN ONE PERSON WEAR?

SHOPPING FREQUENCY

Percent of women who shop for
clothing more than twice a month:

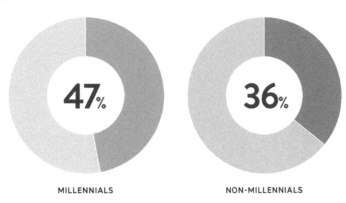

Percent of men who shop for
clothing more than twice a month:

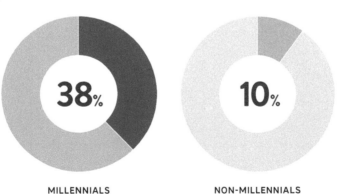

AMOUNT PURCHASED

Millennial women buy 1.33x more
clothes than non-millennial women

Millennial men buy 2x more clothes
than non-millennial men

Source: Boston Consulting Group[8]

WHERE'S THE FREE STUFF?

Whether it's samples at the supermarket or a free desk from the side of the road, everyone loves stuff for free. Luckily, there are all sorts of places to get free things.

Craigslist People give away things for free on Craigslist for all kinds of reasons. Oftentimes, they've already tried to sell the things they're giving away but haven't been successful, or they're moving and need to get rid of it right away.

Freecycle Freecyle is a grassroots movement to connect people who need things with people trying to get rid of things. Check it out, and you might get what you want and keep things out of landfills at the same time.

Product Samples To access freebies, join sites like BzzAgents.com or FreeStuffFinder.com to hook you up with free things.

Credit Card Rewards If you find a rewards credit card with no annual fee and you pay off the full balance of your card every month, the hundreds of dollars in travel rewards that come along with it during the year is like free money.

Rewards Cards If there's a reward card for a store you shop at frequently, take advantage of it. Just don't be tempted to spend money you don't need to spend in order to earn rewards.

HOW CAN BEING FRUGAL SAVE ME MONEY?

A former financial planner, Gary Foreman is the editor and the publisher of *The Dollar Stretcher*, where he dispenses tips that help people live better for less. Here are his suggestions for you.

THREE OF HIS BEST FRUGAL TIPS

1. Make freezer meals. If you are making meatloaf, make extra and put it in the freezer. You can put a meal on the table fairly quickly if you have things prepped in the freezer.

2. Do your own home and car repairs. Now there is so much instruction available online, whether in writing or via videos. Often all you need is a screwdriver and some very basic tools, and you can save a lot of money.

3. Save money on food preparation. We did a study on baby carrots, and we figured out that making them yourself was the equivalent of making $29 an hour. When you're trying to live frugally, you need to make choices that are cheaper, like buying a gallon of bleach instead of a specialty cleaning product that contains bleach.

ON WHAT BEING FRUGAL HAS HELPED HIM ACCOMPLISH "Being frugal has meant I've had less stress in my life. By living frugally, my wife and I were able to build up our savings and pay off all of our student loans while we were still fairly young. That meant that if one of us lost their job we were not in a crisis situation."

ON THE BEST DEAL HE'S EVER GOTTEN "The best deals I've ever gotten are on the things that I didn't buy. Sometimes not buying something is the best choice."

BUT IT'S ON SALE! "We've all fallen for this before. You're out shopping for something very specific when all of a sudden you see a nice T-shirt. You look at it with mild curiosity and then realize it's on sale.

You pick it up and try it on. It looks nice, and so you decide to buy it. At the checkout, you get a little thrill as you calculate how much money you have saved. But have you really saved money? If you didn't need an extra T-shirt, you've actually just spent money you didn't need to spend. There's nothing wrong with buying a T-shirt if it fits into your budget, but we often use the excuse that it was on sale to justify spending more than we intended to. Getting a deal is great, but just being on sale doesn't necessarily make something a smart purchase."

CHAPTER

"BIG" PURCHASES

Life is expensive. Some parts of life are more expensive than others. Whether you're buying a car, a home, or health insurance, you want to make sure you make the right choice. That means it's time to get out your pens and do some pros/cons math.

BUYING A CAR

Millennials have acquired a reputation for being the carless generation. According to a study by CNW Research,[9] Millennials who are 21 to 34 years old buy only 27% of new cars sold. While that might still seem like a lot, that figure peaked in 1985 when young people in that age bracket bought 38% of all new cars. Part of this shift away from car buying is because 32% of Millennials live in cities, which is more than any other generation according to a 2009 report by Pew Research Center.[10] In cities with access to public transit, cars are often an unnecessary expense. Despite this, some predict that Millennials will start buying more cars as they get older and start making more money. Whether you're on the older end of the spectrum or just one of those Millennials searching for a car, here are a few of the things you'll need to consider.

Buy or Lease The first decision that many people agonize over is whether to buy or lease a car. If you lease the car, you will have lower monthly payments and can choose another car to lease in a few years—guaranteeing that you always have a new car. For people who depend heavily on their cars, this can often be comforting; they feel like there's less chance of having to deal with costly and stressful repairs.

Leasing can make sense also if you own your own business or freelance. Leasing a car can potentially save you some money since the depreciation and interest of a leased car can be used as a tax deduction. If you buy the car with a loan, you won't be able to deduct it.

The problem with leasing a car is that it almost always works out to cost you more in the long run than buying a car outright or with a car loan. The reason is because the costs of a car decrease every year you own it. Financially, you're far better off buying a car and keeping it for a long time than leasing new cars every few years.

Pay Cash or Finance Cash is definitely king. Since not having to pay interest keeps your overall costs lower, it is far better to purchase a car outright than with a loan. However, for many people that's impossible to do since they just don't have the cash available. If that's the case, look around for the best deal you can find on interest rates—and don't let the

DON'T FALL FOR 0% FINANCING

Zero percent financing sounds like a great deal. You get to buy a car with a loan, but you don't have to pay any interest? Who wouldn't want that? The problem is that 0% interest is often offered as just one of the many incentives you can choose from. Many of these deals have terrible stipulations. In some, you can't negotiate on the price of the car if you take the 0% deal. Read the fine print and do what's best for you. Finally, 0% financing often applies only to the cars currently on the lot, which means your options will be limited in terms of colors, models and other features. That might mean you might end up paying more for extra features you don't need because that's all that's available.

car salesman distract you with the promise of low weekly or monthly payments. These "easy low payments" are often a tactic salesmen use to sell you a car that is more expensive than you can afford. To get around the fact that it's above your price range, they extend the payments for a longer period of time, falsely making the car seem affordable. Before you sign on any dotted line, do the math to see how much you will be paying over the course of the loan, including interest. Make a choice that is right for you based on the facts, not the spin.

New or Used One of the most hotly debated questions among those buying a car is whether to buy a new or used one. There are a few very compelling reasons to buy used over new. For one, used cars are considerably less expensive. According to *AutoTrader*,[11] it's estimated that in the first year of ownership a car loses an average of 30% of its value. That means that if you were to buy a new model, it would cost $30,000, whereas if you were to buy a car that was only one year old, you would pay around $20,000. That's a significant difference. Another way you'll save by buying used is on car insurance. Older cars are worth less, making them cheaper to insure.

Many dealerships now offer extended warranties that either come with the car or that can be purchased for an additional fee. Also, depending on how old the car you purchase is, it might still have some time or distance left on its manufacturer's warranty.

WHAT TO LOOK FOR IF YOU'RE BUYING USED

When you find a car you like, be sure to get a vehicle history report on it. These can easily be obtained through websites like Carfax or Auto-Check and they provide you with information like the car's accident history and more. Also, ask if the seller has a record of regular maintenance on the car. If a car has been well-maintained it will be more likely to last and keep its value longer. Cars that have lower mileage are also generally better. Finally, make sure that you won't need to pay for any expensive repairs in the near future by determining the wear on the tires and the brakes. If you can, have a mechanic do an evaluation before buying it.

Despite all the benefits of buying a used car, many people still buy new cars. For some people, the only way they can qualify for financing is to buy a new car. Other people just love the opportunity to choose the features they want. Still others like the peace of mind they get from buying new. Do what's right for you and your budget.

Choosing a Vehicle There are so many options available when you're in the market for a new car. Make a list of all the things that you want in your car; decide which are deal breakers and which aren't. Once you have a list of the things you're looking for, you can go out and see what's on the market. If you're looking for used cars, try to give yourself plenty of time to find exactly what you need. You don't want to feel pressured to buy something that isn't right. See Table 13 for info on cars with the best resale value.

IN THE FIRST YEAR OF OWNERSHIP, A CAR LOSES ON AVERAGE 30% OF ITS VALUE

TABLE 13
CARS WITH THE BEST RESALE VALUES

Not all cars are created equal. Not only are some cars less likely to break down or to need costly repairs, but they also depreciate slower than others, which means that you'll lose less value over the years you own your car. According to Consumer Reports, these are your best bets:

COST	SMALL CAR	SEDAN	SUV
Less than $10,000	Toyota Prius (2004 to 2007)	Hyundai Sonata (2007 to 2008)	Toyota High-lander V6 (2004)
$10,000 to $15,000	Honda Fit (2011 to 2013)	Mazda3 (2009 to 2012)	Acura MDX (2004 to 2006)
$15,000 to $20,000	Hyundai Elantra (2012 to 2013)	Toyota Camry (2011 to 2012)	Lexus RX (2006 to 2007)
$20,000 to $25,000	N/A	Toyota Avalon (2011)	Toyota High-lander Hybrid (2008 to 2009)

Source: Consumer Reports[12]

BUYING A HOUSE

The allure of owning your own home is powerful. When you rent, you can't truly put down roots. Everything is temporary and potentially in flux. Your landlord might decide they won't be renting the place any longer. You don't want to paint or make any changes because you'll have to change everything back when you move. You don't want to buy expensive furniture because it might not fit into your next place. Still, for many Millennials, buying a home just isn't a priority (see Figure 6).

FIGURE 6

OWNING A HOME ISN'T A PRIORITY

Owning a home isn't that big a priority for Millennials. A recent study by Pew Research placed it fourth on the list of what is most important in their lives:

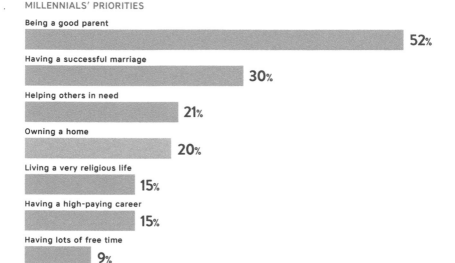

MILLENNIALS' PRIORITIES

Being a good parent
52%

Having a successful marriage
30%

Helping others in need
21%

Owning a home
20%

Living a very religious life
15%

Having a high-paying career
15%

Having lots of free time
9%

Becoming famous
1%

Source: Pew Social Trends[13]

Buying a home can be a good investment. You might be sick of paying your landlord's mortgage every month. In some places, it can actually only cost a little more money to buy than it does to rent. Still, things can go wrong. House prices could fall significantly, leaving you with a mortgage that's more than your house is worth. In fact, many experts don't suggest you buy a house unless you're certain that you will live in it for at least 10 years.

If you're thinking about buying a home, the first thing you need to determine is if you can afford to buy. The general rule of thumb is that you should spend around 30% of your gross income on housing costs. That includes insurance, property taxes, utilities, and maintenance.

Even if your costs come to 30% or less, make sure you can afford that 30%. If you have fixed expenses every month, whatever leftover you usually have will help you determine how much you can afford to spend on a house.

WHERE IN AMERICA SHOULD YOU LIVE?

Should you follow the artists and move to dirt-cheap downtown Detroit? Or should you go to a place where you're more likely to take home a big paycheck, like San Francisco? Choosing where you live can often feel like a catch-22. If you choose a place based on affordability, you're more likely to move someplace where you'll have a harder time finding a job. Meanwhile if you choose a place where the economy is booming, you'll likely have to pay for inflated living costs. According to Trulia, the five most affordable housing markets are located in Ohio, Indiana, and upstate New York, but these areas have fewer economic opportunities. *The Atlantic* recently looked at places where affordability and opportunity intersect and found Pittsburgh, Minneapolis, and Salt Lake City to be great places for Millennials to move to.[14]

The next thing you should gauge is if you have enough money set aside to put toward a down payment. Putting down 20% or more will allow you to avoid having to purchase expensive things like private mortgage insurance, will increase your likelihood of getting approved for a mortgage, and will decrease your monthly mortgage payment. Remember, you shouldn't put all your savings toward a down payment.

Get Pre-Approved for a Mortgage   The first step to getting a mortgage is pre-approval. That means it's time to put your best suit on, get all your paperwork in order, and head down to the bank to smooth-talk your future mortgage broker. Or, you can stay home in your PJs and apply online. Getting pre-approved can help you estimate how much you can afford to spend on your new home and give you an idea of whether you'll even qualify for a mortgage.

Prove Your Income   Mortgage brokers will want everything you tell them about your financial picture to be proven or backed up. That means you need to bring things like your W-2 statement from the past two years, your last two tax returns, pay stubs that will show your income during recent pay periods plus your year-to-date income, and also proof of any additional income you receive, including bonuses, tips, child support or alimony, or earnings from part-time business.

Prove Your Assets You will need to bring bank statements and statements from your investments accounts. Your lender will want to know where the money for your down payment will be coming from. If your parents or anyone else is helping you out, you will need a letter saying that their contributions will be a gift and not a loan.

You Will Need to Verify Everything They will check your credit score, your employer, your salary, and your Social Security number. You will need to bring your driver's license and your Social Security card.

What If You Have Bad Credit? If you have bad credit, there are things you can do to increase your chances of getting approved for a mortgage. The first thing to do is to work to improve your credit score. For ideas on how to do so, check out Chapter 9.

The next thing you can do is decrease the debt you currently have. Lenders are wary of offering mortgages to people who have a high debt-to-income ratio. While you can also tweak this ratio by increasing your income, according to Zillow.com decreasing your debt so that the ratio is 36% or under will also help you qualify for a mortgage.[15] In fact, the Consumer Financial Protection Bureau, a government organization, now insists that you can't have more than a 43% debt-to-income ratio[16] for a qualified mortgage. That means that all of your mortgage, property tax, and debt payments can't add up to more than 43% of what you make every month.

Keep the Market in Mind You'll almost always find one or two homes that have been on the market forever. They're reasonably priced, but no one is making an offer because they have weird features or awkward layouts or are completely outdated. You might be able to get them for a steal, but if you can't easily fix the reason why buyers shied away from them, you'll also be faced with a hard time selling when the time comes.

When you're buying your home, think about what the next buyer will think about it. Two-bedroom and three-bedroom homes generally sell best in most markets because there are more potential buyers. If houses in particularly good school districts are known for selling well, consider buying in that school district. Find out what motivates buyers in your area and buy a home that will be easy to unload.

THE UPS AND DOWNS OF THE REAL ESTATE MARKET

It's important to understand how the real estate market works if you want to buy a home. The first thing to understand is that real estate markets generally operate on regional levels. They are underpinned by the local economy, local job prospects, and local median salaries. The stronger the local economy, the higher local housing prices will generally be. Interest rates also play a key role. When interest rates rise, the cost of a mortgage increases, making the demand and price of real estate decrease. When interest rates fall, the cost of a mortgage decreases, and thus property prices and demand will often increase. The overall health of the national economy also has an impact; some economists predict demographic shifts like boomers retiring to condos will make a difference in the near future.

Buy a Home That Needs a Little Work A home that isn't completely updated might not meet all of your needs right away, but with a little paint and elbow grease, you can potentially make it into your dream home (see Table 14). Even if you shy away from DIY, you could have professionals make changes. Just be sure not to take on more than you can handle.

Look for Things That Will Save You Money Not all homes are created equal. If the home has solar panels, it will most likely save you a lot of money on your electric bills. A home that is properly insulated will save you a significant amount of money on your energy bills. If a home has recently had the roof or furnace replaced, that will save you the expense of replacing them. Look for updates, repairs, or energy efficiencies that the current owners have taken care of.

Stay Within Your Budget It's so tempting to break your home-buying budget when you walk into a dream home priced just out of your range. Unless you can easily afford the extra amount, stick to your original budget. Living in your dream house won't be a dream if you're stressed out about money all the time.

Get a Full Home Inspection Get a complete home inspection before you buy a house. Sure, you probably won't find a snake infestation, but you might find something like toxic mold, dangerous wiring, or a buckling foundation. Save yourself future headaches and know ahead of time what you're getting into.

Make an Offer You've made extensive lists about what you need in your dream home, looked at dozens of homes, and now you've found the one that's right for you. Now it's time to make an offer.

To get an idea of how much to offer, look at previous sales of similar properties in the area. How much they sold for will give you a better idea of the range that you should consider. If many of them sold below asking, it indicates that you might potentially succeed with a similar offer.

You should also look at how long the house has been on the market. The longer the house has been for sale, the more motivated sellers usually are to see it sell quickly.

Negotiate the Offer and Satisfy Any Conditions Most homeowners won't just accept your first offer. Often they will try to negotiate for more money. You can potentially ask for more here as well. If the appliances aren't included in the original offer, you might ask for them in exchange for more money. Make sure to get everything that will be included in the sale in the contract and include the conditions on which the sale will be completed. Some buyers include the condition that they will sell their current home. You'll also have to decide when you will get possession of the house. Typically people take possession 30 to 90 days from the signing of the contract.

Get Your Mortgage Once you've agreed on all the conditions and had your home inspected, you need to go back to your mortgage broker to apply for your mortgage (see Table 15, page 120, for types of mortgages). Remember, being pre-approved is no guarantee that your mortgage application will be approved. It is also time to start getting your down payment ready and shopping for insurance.

Move Moving is stressful when you're renting, but it can be even more stressful when you're buying a home. On top of everything else happening the day you take possession of your new home, you will also need

TABLE 14

HOME IMPROVEMENTS THAT WILL PUT MONEY IN YOUR POCKET

IMPROVEMENT	WHY
Add Moldings	Everyone wants crown moldings these days. Add some pizzazz to your floor boards and ceilings.
Stick to Neutrals	Garish paint colors turn buyers off. They'll pay more if the paint colors stick to a simple palette.
Change the Front Door	It's the first thing you see. Either paint or replace the front door and see the price of your place increase.
Open Up the Space	The modern homebuyer wants an open plan and knocking down unnecessary walls will help make your home seem bigger.
Floors	Homebuyers like laminate or wood flooring. Get rid of your carpeting or tile.
Landscaping	Landscaping makes your home have nicer curb appeal and ensures a proper first impression.

to go to the property and do a walk-through to make sure everything is according to the contract. If anything isn't, you will need to note it so the seller can fix it.

Live Happily Ever After Now that you've found, bought, and moved into your dream home, it's time to live happily ever after. Hopefully, you will have many happy years there. Unfortunately, it doesn't always work this way.

TABLE 15

WHAT TYPE OF MORTGAGE DO YOU WANT?

TYPE OF MORTGAGE	WHAT IT MEANS
Fixed Rate Mortgages	The interest rate remains the same over the course of your mortgage. This is a good choice when interest rates are low since you lock in a low rate.
Variable Rate Mortgages	This interest rate varies over the course of your mortgage according to the market. If interest rates are high, then this will allow for decreases in rates. When interest rates are low, the variable rate will often be lower than the fixed rate, but over the life of the loan you will probably pay more in interest.
Balloon Mortgage	This loan is a risky loan. It is a fixed rate mortgage with low payments, but then after a period of time, the balance is due.
Interest-Only Mortgage	This is also a risky loan. You only pay interest on the loan, and then like a balloon mortgage, the loan is due.
Federal Housing Association Loan (FHA)	If you're a first-time buyer and have a low income, you'll only need to put 3% to 5% down.
VA Loan	If you're serving in the military or the spouse of a deceased military vet, you won't need a down payment or you will only need a small one.
USDA Loan	If you have low income and are buying in a rural area, you qualify. No down payment or mortgage insurance.

WALKING AWAY FROM A MORTGAGE

When you buy a home, you never imagine the day that you won't be able to afford your payment. Sometimes that day comes, and walking away from a mortgage might seem like the best option. If fact, some people strategically default when changes in housing prices mean they owe more on their homes than their homes are worth. Still, the American Bankers Association[17] warns that having a foreclosure on your credit report will drop your FICO score by 100 to 400 points, and it may take anywhere from three to seven years to qualify for a new mortgage. Taxes might also be due on the unpaid debt since it is treated as income; you could be taken to court for any difference between the amount that the bank got from selling your home and what you owe.

BUYING HEALTH INSURANCE

We all know at least one story of someone unexpectedly getting sick when they're not covered by insurance or they have substandard coverage. Don't let that be you. It's just not worth it. To make the right choice, understand your options.

Level of Coverage When you're shopping for health insurance from your state's marketplace, you will first see that plans are organized based on the level of coverage that they offer you.

- Platinum: Covers 90% of costs
- Gold: Covers 80% of costs
- Silver: Covers 70% of costs
- Bronze: Covers 60% of costs
- Catastrophic or High-Deductible Health Plan: Only covers expenses after you've met a high deductible

Obviously, plans that cover a higher percentage of costs will have higher monthly premiums. If you're relatively healthy, you might choose to spend less every month on premiums and take the chance that you won't need any expensive procedures—procedures for which your copays will be significant.

The next thing you will have to do is choose a type of plan. There are four main types.

Health Maintenance Organization (HMO) An HMO provides medical services to you from a network of professionals. While you benefit by having lower premiums, no deductibles, smaller copays, less paperwork, and more predictable costs, if you see a doctor outside your network, you will have to pay the bill yourself unless it's an emergency. You will also have a primary care physician who you must go through in order to access other services.

Preferred Provider Organization (PPO) While a PPO also has a network of doctors, unlike an HMO, you can also see doctors outside your network; you'll just have to pay a little more if you do. PPOs have higher copays than HMOs, and some have deductibles. The premiums for PPOs also tend to be higher than HMOs.

Point-of-Service Plan (POS) POS plans give you freedom to choose your doctors. Like an HMO, you will have a primary care physician who will coordinate your care. Similar to a PPO, you can see doctors who are outside your network, but you will have to pay more. The premiums of a POS plan are often lower than PPO plans, but you'll often have higher copays.

High-Deductible Health Plan (HDHP) With a HDHP you still choose from an HMO, PPO, and POS, but they don't begin to cover you until your costs exceed a very high deductible with the exception of preventative care. The deductibles change each year, but for 2015, the highest deductible that you could have is $6,450 for an individual and $12,900 for a family, and the lowest deductible you could have is $1,300 for an individual and $2,600 for a family. Once you've reached your deductible, your plan kicks in. Many people who get this plan also get an HSA and save pre-tax dollars toward their health care costs. These plans have the lowest premiums.

YOU CAN'T DUCT-TAPE A BROKEN ARM, AND OTHER REASONS YOU NEED INSURANCE

Health insurance is expensive, but that doesn't mean you shouldn't get it. According to *InsuranceQuotes.org*, even with the Affordable Care Act one in four Americans aged 18 to 29 does not have health insurance.[18] In fact, Millennials are two times more likely not to have health insurance than any other age group. While it might be tempting to skip on the expensive monthly premiums if you're relatively healthy, you never know what life has in store for you. I like being alive, and I'm sure you do too. Get insurance so that if something really bad happens you're covered.

COBRA Also known as Consolidated Omnibus Budget Reconciliation Act. The reason it's important for you to know about COBRA is that if you get laid off from your employer, you will lose the health insurance coverage you are currently getting through them. That can be very disruptive to your medical coverage. Luckily, the government recognized this and did something about it. COBRA allows you to continue paying your former employer's portion of your health benefits, keeping your coverage and the attractive group rates that your employer is most likely getting. COBRA won't cover you forever, but it will cover you for around 18 months, with the possibility of extending up to 36 months. Hopefully, by that time you will have another employer!

DON'T GO UNINSURED—IT'S JUST NOT WORTH IT

ADVICE FOR BIG PURCHASES

When you're spending thousands of dollars on a big purchase, you want to be sure you're making the right decision. You might even want to seek out an expert to help you. To give you advice, I sought out David Ning, the founder of the popular blog *MoneyNing*. David is a published author and entrepreneur whose frugal tips and personal finance advice attract upward of 500,000 readers to his blog every month. Here are his best tips when it comes to big purchases.

HIS ADVICE FOR BUYING A CAR "Paying cash is always great, but I understand that most people will end up leasing theirs. When trying to negotiate the payments, make sure to completely understand all the terms. Other than the price of the car, there are many line items, such as the money factor, that can be negotiated to lower the total costs of owning that car. And don't just look at the monthly costs, but rather the total costs of owning your ride."

HIS ADVICE FOR BUYING YOUR FIRST HOME "Start slow. Understand your finances, your preferences, and your long-term goals. Know that all those dream homes you see that are out of your price range will become just "your home" once you move in and get used to it while you dream for something even nicer and better. Try hard to avoid the urge to buy a house that's too big for your family or your budget. You don't want to be working for your house the rest of your life."

HIS ADVICE FOR BUYING HEALTH INSURANCE "Pencil out the numbers. For many, the lower payment with high-deductible plans will be the cheapest. But don't forget the out-of-pocket costs either. Add it all up and find the option that is the least expensive once you factor in the tax credits, FSAs, and other subsidies. It's a big hassle, but the wrong choice can be pretty costly too."

ON MISTAKES TO AVOID MAKING "Don't put things on credit, of course, but try your best not to buy just to impress others either. That luxury factor can be really expensive, and the difference between a functional brand versus that luxury brand only grows larger as the prices get higher."

ON HACKS TO HELP YOU SAVE ON BIG PURCHASES "Can you share the costs with someone or rent it if it's an item you don't need all the time? Can you make money from the purchase, like renting out a room if you buy a place? Do you really need it? There are specific tips for every purchase, so search the web to see how others are getting more for less money. You'll be surprised how much a small time investment can yield in cost savings."

HACKS

DON'T GET THE CONTRACT

If you're not sure how much you're going to use a service like a gym membership, wait and see before you sign up for a long-term contract. Businesses love signing you up for contracts that you never use; but often you're better off paying per use for a service or product rather than buying a subscription or annual membership.

GIVE TO CHARITY AND GET BACK FROM THE IRS

You know how people often say that the more you give the more you'll get back? That's true when it comes to taxes. When you donate money or items in-kind to a charity, you qualify for a tax exemption. Make sure to keep a record of your donations and claim them when tax season comes around. If you volunteer for a charity, you can also claim mileage and some expenses for travel. While the IRS will only give you 14 cents a mile, they will also pay for parking or tolls needed to get you to

your volunteer commitment. If you want to make slightly larger gifts (>$250) to charity, consider giving it in terms of appreciated stock. This is how the 1% make their charitable contributions, because their expensive lawyers and accountants know that it will give them the best deductions. By giving appreciated stock, you don't have to pay capital gains and you can give more and get a bigger deduction.

UNEXPECTED EXPENSES

What do you do when you have an unexpected expense that completely blows your budget? If you have an emergency fund, then it's time to tap into that. If not, then you should try to find a way to avoid putting it on your credit card. Perhaps it means putting off buying something else you were planning to buy or maybe it means deciding to cut back on going out to eat and other entertainment costs. You might want to try living for a few weeks off what you have in your pantry and cupboards rather than go grocery shopping. Or maybe you can sell a few things around your house you don't need anymore or take on a part-time job or side hustle. Once your budget recovers, be sure to add a category for emergencies or unexpected expenses so that you can handle these expenses better in the future.

WHY FREE ISN'T FREE

Many marketers try to sell you their products by offering them to you for free. Whether it's three months free cable or one month free high-speed Internet, they're trying to get you to sign a contract, get hooked on the service, or forget to cancel the subscription before they charge you for it. Don't sign up for the free service unless you actually want it and can afford it. If you want the freebie but don't want to pay for it, make sure to put a note in your calendar to remind yourself to cancel the service before you're charged.

CALCULATE COST-PER-USE

Before you buy a new piece of clothing or any other item, consider calculating how much it will cost you each time you use it. You get to this number by estimating how many times you'll use it and dividing the price you pay by this number. If you pay $100 for a coat or dress and only wear it three times, it has cost you $33 each time you've worn it. Those evenings better have been worth that price! By calculating how much you'll pay per use, you'll be more likely to make decisions that provide you with more value for your money.

WHY BUYING CHEAP IS BAD

Sometimes a good deal isn't really worth it. If what you're buying will receive a lot of wear and tear, spend a little more money and buy better quality. You'll be much better off buying one $150 coat that will last five years than two $75 coats that fall apart.

THE TRUE COST OF "FREE" APPS

Some of the best apps are free. You can download them to your phone at no cost to you, and you can start using them. But after you realize how much fun that video game is or how useful that app is, you get asked to make an in-app purchase or to upgrade your app to the professional version. It might start innocently enough. You'll be playing Candy Crush, and you'll pay a few dollars for an extra chance to beat a level, but these costs quickly add up.

This is great for app developers since the likelihood that you would've spent several hundred dollars on a mobile video game is quite low. But by offering you an app for free and getting you hooked, they're able to make much more money off of you. You would have been much better off buying a video game app for five dollars that doesn't have in-app purchases than getting a free app. Luckily, you can easily get free alternatives to most apps that you're currently paying money for. If you're already addicted to an app like Candy Crush, set a budget for how much you're willing to spend per month on in-app purchases and stick to it.

CREATE A CASH FLOW MAP

If you want to be a bazillionaire, you need to stop living paycheck-to-paycheck and start spending less than you earn. That means making a budget and ensuring you're sticking to it every month. This is harder for people who freelance, are self-employed, or have a side hustle, since the amount of money you might make every month varies depending on how much work you do that month, or on your clients' payment schedules. To ensure that you can meet all your financial goals and obligations, you should be tracking your expected cash flow so that you can anticipate those times when money will be tight and do something beforehand to deal with the problem.

If you don't have a clear idea of when money will be coming in and going out, you'll be more likely to rely on credit cards. By having a clear picture, you can negotiate your contracts to better meet your needs in terms of cash flow, and potentially put off expenses until you will have sufficient funds to cover them.

BEAT BANK TRICKS

Everyone is looking out for "number one," and banks are no different. Be careful when using your debit card when your checking account is low on funds. Many merchants like gas stations and hotels place authorization holds on your accounts that are much higher than what you actually spend. For example, if you have $49 in your bank account and you put $20 in gas in your car, you might be charged overdraft fees by your bank since the gas station put a $50 authorization hold on your card. The money is never spent, but your bank might charge you for the overdraft fees regardless. Banks will also sometimes reorder your transactions in order to send you into overdraft more quickly by ensuring the largest transactions are taken off your account balance first rather than in the order that you purchased things. If your bank does this, call and complain and they might remove the fees.

HOW TO SAVE ON IN VITRO FERTILIZATION (IVF)

Not being able to conceive is devastating. For those who want to have their own biological children, IVF is an option, but it's expensive. In fact, The American Society of Reproductive Medicine lists the average cost of one IVF cycle at $12,400.[19] Since each round only has a 20% to 40% success rate, most couples need more than one round of IVF. While some insurance plans cover IVF, they often don't cover the full costs or they just cover the first round. If you do need IVF, then you might want to consider setting up a health savings account or starting a crowdsourcing campaign to help you save the money. You can also potentially go somewhere where IVF is cheaper like the Czech Republic or the UK or Canada, where you can save thousands of dollars per cycle.

You can also potentially get a loan for the procedure or apply for an IVF scholarship.

PAY YOUR CAR INSURANCE IN A LUMP SUM

Paying your car insurance in a lump sum is almost always the best way to go. By choosing to pay monthly, your insurance company will charge you a financing fee, which can be anywhere from 3% to 5% of the cost of your insurance. While it's not an enormous amount, depending on how much you're paying for your insurance it can add up. You won't be able to make that much money in interest if your money is sitting in a savings account anyway, so do yourself a favor and pay it all at once.

BUY THINGS AT THE END OF THE SEASON

There is an optimal time to buy things in order to take advantage of the best prices. If you wait too long to buy a swimsuit, for example, not only will there be little selection left, but also it might mean you have to go to a specialty swimwear shop where swimwear tends to be more expensive. August is the best time to buy summer clothing, and after Christmas and early January tends to be the best time to buy fall and winter wear, when many stores restock with new lines of winter clothes. That second restock of winter wear tends to go on sale in March, when stores start stocking for spring, and spring wear tends to go on sale in April and May, when the summer stock comes out. If you do happen to need a swimsuit in November and you are having a hard time finding one, check out an outlet mall and you might just find a great deal.

DON'T BE FOOLED BY BLACK FRIDAY

Is it worth it to stand in line for hours for a Black Friday deal? Not usually. Stores might be advertising cheap TVs, but make sure to do your research. Sometimes, they only have a few TVs per store and hundreds of people will be lining up waiting for the same prize. More often, the TVs being advertised aren't even usually carried in the store as they are of lesser quality. Also, remember that even if the discount is amazing, in all likelihood they will be offering discounts that are almost as good in the weeks leading up to the holidays. While you might think you scored a great deal by standing outside in the freezing cold for hours, won't you feel dumb when you realize that you only really saved $50 more than you might have if you had waited?

CATCH THE TRAVEL GLITCHES

How does a $43 flight from New York to Hong Kong sound? Or a $7 Business Class flight to anywhere within Europe? Too good to be true? Travel glitches happen to even the best airlines, and many of them actually honor the prices that they accidentally charge. That means that if you can buy them before the airline realizes what's happened and changes the price, you can get some very cheap travel. Since travel glitches come and go quite quickly, you'll have to act fast. Stay up-to-date by joining online forums like FlyerTalk and FatWallet, which have threads that monitor travel glitches.

ASK FOR THE MANAGER

Whenever you're calling a customer service helpline to complain or try to negotiate a better deal, always ask to speak to the manager first. Customer service representatives aren't authorized to do very much. You will waste your time if you spend too long trying to get them to give you what you want. You want to talk to someone who actually has the power to negotiate with you. Once you do get the manager on the phone, make sure you're nice even if you're calling to complain. You're more likely to get them to give you what you want if you're kind and calm. At some companies, however, asking for the manager isn't enough. If the manager isn't helpful, then ask for the customer retention department. People working in these departments are empowered to do everything they can to keep you as a customer—and they often have the most latitude for granting your requests.

BUY CHEAP GIFT CARDS

Have you ever gotten a gift card you know you'll never use? So has everyone else. But some people resell those cards instead of sticking them in their wallets and forgetting about them. Consider reducing your monthly costs or getting a discount on a special purchase by buying gift cards from resellers for stores you're planning on shopping at anyways. Someone else's crummy gift card just might be exactly what you need to save some extra money since these resold gift cards are almost always sold at a discount. While discounts generally start at 10% for popular gift cards, some sell for as little as 50% of their face value, including cards for businesses like Starbucks.

While you can purchase gift cards on sites like eBay and Craigslist, opt for buying them through an official reseller like Cardpool.com and PlasticJungle.com. You can also use those sites to sell all your unwanted cards and free up some space in your wallet.

GET FIT WITH YOUTUBE

Whether it's a yoga class or a high-intensity interval training (HIIT) workout, classes keep your workout varied and interesting. But fitness classes are expensive. Turn to YouTube for your fitness classes. Not only can you work out in the comfort of your home, but you do so for free. Whether you like Pilates, yoga, Zumba, HIIT, or strength building, there's something for you on YouTube. Some fun fitness channels include Scott Herman Fitness, SparkPeople, PopSugar Fitness, Tara Stiles, Blogilates, Yogasync. tv, and BexLife.

BUY MORE VERSATILE CLOTHING

Rather than buying into the latest trends, consider buying clothing in more classic styles and accessorizing with trendy accessories. Consider buying clothing to wear during the summer that easily transitions to fall. There are some styles of summer dresses and shirts that are just too summery to be worn in layers when it gets colder. Instead of buying something that can only be worn during one season, buy a piece of clothing that is more versatile and can easily be worn underneath a sweater or under a blazer. This will mean you'll purchase fewer clothes.

BOOK TRAVEL AT THE RIGHT TIME

Everyone wants to get the best deal on plane tickets, but most people believe that finding a great price is a matter of chance. Luckily, CheapAir.com studied when plane tickets were the cheapest and discovered that there's a secret to getting the best deal.[20] The study, which took place in 2013, analyzed 4 million flights and found that you'll get the best deal if you book an average of 54 days before your flight for a domestic trip within the United States. They also analyzed the optimal time to book your flight for a number of other destinations.[21] These included:

South Pacific: 70 days before
Mexico: 89 days before
Latin America: 80 days before
Asia: 129 days before
Africa: 166 days before
Caribbean: 101 days before
Europe: 151 days before
Middle East: 80 days before

Another study by FareCompare[22] analyzed what day of the week and time of day were the best for booking flights, and they found that Tuesday at 3:00 p.m. EST was ideal. They also found that early-morning or late-night flights were cheaper, and that value-minded travelers should book flights for Wednesdays, Tuesdays, or Saturdays, and avoid booking on Friday and Sunday since those are the most expensive days to fly.

STOP IMPULSE BUYING

Companies design their stores so that the things you want most are the hardest to find or located the furthest from the entrance. For example, at a grocery store it's not an accident that things like milk, eggs, and butter are often located near the back. The goal is to get you to walk past all sorts of other temptations to increase your likelihood of buying more than just what you need. Some hacks that help you cut down on buying things you don't need include shopping with your spouse and not using a shopping cart at the grocery store, since you might psychologically feel the need to fill it up.

SEE THROUGH THE DISCOUNT

Stores often advertise heavy discounts of 50% to 75% off. That gives you the perception that because of the sale, you have a special opportunity to save a significant amount of money, and if you miss that opportunity, you will have to pay 50% to 75% more. That leads you to feel like you're getting a better deal than you might be, and provides an incentive for you to act quickly and buy. But often these aren't actual 75% off deals, since the regular price is rarely if ever actually asked. There are certain clothing retailers, for example, that send out weekly emails advertising a new sale where you can get 40% to 50% off the whole store. Before you get excited about a big sale, ask yourself whether you're really getting such a significant discount or if that discount is partly being manipulated in order to make the deal seem more attractive.

DON'T LET THEM SCARE YOU

Advertisements often appeal to our deepest fears. Whether they are trying to peddle antibacterial spray by evoking the fear of getting sick, or expensive face creams by evoking the fear of aging, many people are motivated by those fears to do exactly what the advertisers want—buy their products. The next time you find yourself thinking about buying something because you're scared of what might happen if you don't, take a step back and really consider if you need that product.

BEFORE YOU BUY SOMETHING, POST ABOUT IT

Need a tent or a cooler? Why buy one when you can borrow one? Social media is a great way to quickly and easily ask a bunch of your friends if they have that ladder or power tool that they can lend you. If you only need to use something once or very occasionally, it makes a lot more sense to just borrow it off someone you know than to buy it and have it sit around. Even if you make them dinner or buy them a beer to thank them, you'll usually be financially ahead and you will have spent your money on your friend and not an item taking up space in your storage locker or basement. If no one you know is willing or able to lend you the thing you need, then they might be able to suggest where you can buy it or a make or model that has worked well for them. I've made some of my best buying decisions thanks to recommendations I've gotten from friends on Facebook.

PART

BORROWING IT

CHAPTER

CREDIT: SCORES, REPORTS, HISTORY

Credit scores seem mysterious and inscrutable things. In the United States, everyone with a credit history is scored based on factors that assess credit-worthiness. According to the American Bankers Association, however, more than half of Americans don't know their own credit scores.[23] And when they do know them, they usually don't understand them. In this chapter, we'll look at everything you need to know about credit scores.

WHAT IS IT?

A credit score is a three-digit number that rates each individual on how well they have managed credit. This number is calculated based on your credit report and helps lenders determine how risky it is to lend you money. In fact, your credit score can determine whether you'll get approved for a loan, a mortgage, or a credit card, as well as what interest rate you'll be charged.

Here's where it gets complicated: All of us have more than one credit score. In fact, there are hundreds of credit scores; different institutions calculate and score consumers differently. Despite the existence of so many different scores, when we talk about credit scores, we're usually talking about a FICO score. In fact, according to FICO, 90% of the 100 largest financial institutions use this score. Other commonly talked-about scores are "educational scores," given out by the three biggest credit reporting bureaus: Equifax, Transunion, and Experian.

A FICO score ranges from 300 to 850 points. If your FICO score is 850, then you have a perfect score. According to Experian, a good score is above 700 and an amazing score is above 750.[24] A bad credit score is 580 and below, and if you have a score under 500, you will have a lot of difficulty opening any credit accounts.[25] Where do most people find themselves in that mix? According to FICO, the median score is 723.

HOW IS IT CALCULATED?

According to FICO, your score is calculated based on five main factors (see Figure 7).

Payment History Your payment history makes up 35% of your FICO score. Things like late payments, foreclosures, bankruptcy, liens, judgments, settlements, charge-offs, and repossessions will cause this part of your score to drop. To get a good score in this area, you have to fulfill your debt obligations by making payments on time and in full.

FIGURE 7

FICO'S CREDIT SCORE CALCULATION UNMASKED

Your credit score calculation might seem complicated, but it breaks down fairly simply into the categories below:

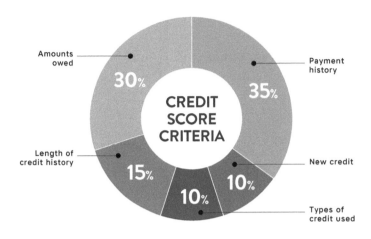

Source: FICO[26]

Debt Burden Debt burden makes up 30% of your score. According to FICO, there are six different metrics that fall under this rubric, including the total amount you owe on all accounts, how many accounts have balances, how much is owed on different accounts, how much debt you have in relation to your credit limit, the amount you've paid down on any loans, and the amount owed across your various accounts.

Length of Credit History This part of your FICO score counts for 15% and measures how long you have had a credit history. In general, if you have a longer credit history, this part of your credit score will be higher. This section takes into account when your first credit account was established, how long you have had your current accounts, the length of time you've had your newest credit account, and the average age of all your credit accounts. It also factors in the last time you used your current accounts.

Types of Credit Used This part of your FICO score accounts for 10% of your score and looks at the mix of your credit accounts. It will take into consideration if you have credit cards, a mortgage, student loans, and retail loans. It's good to have at least one credit card in this mix; those without a history of managing credit cards responsibly are considered a higher credit risk.

Recent Searches and New Accounts This 10% of your score looks at how many times a lender has requested your credit report or score. If you check your own credit score, this will not impact your FICO. While having one or two lenders check your score doesn't have a huge impact, if you have opened or applied for a number of new accounts during a short period of time, it could work against you. People who try to open many new accounts in a short period of time are often treated as bad credit risks since this usually occurs when an individual is experiencing financial difficulties.

WHAT'S THE DIFFERENCE BETWEEN A CREDIT SCORE, REPORT, AND HISTORY?

In addition to your credit score, there are things like your credit history and your credit report to learn about. It can sometimes be difficult to understand the nuances between the three.

Your credit history is used to calculate your credit score. It is a listing of all the credit information that has been collected about you. This includes everything about every account you've ever had, how much money you've borrowed and repaid, if you've paid it on time, and if you've had any problem paying back money that you've borrowed. While lenders often use your credit score to decide whether or not to lend to you, they usually also look at your credit history as a way of understanding more about you. The credit score is the summary, whereas your credit history is the full picture. See Table 16 for how much a bad score can hurt you.

TABLE 16
THE TRUE COST OF A BAD CREDIT SCORE

If you don't have a good credit score, you won't get the best interest rates. How much will paying higher interest rates cost you over the course of a thirty-year fixed-rate mortgage? According to myFICO.com loan calculator, this is how much you'll pay depending on your credit score.

FICO SCORE	APR	MONTHLY PAYMENT	TOTAL INTEREST PAID
760–850	3.492%	$1,121	$153,738
700–759	3.714%	$1,153	$164,968
680–699	3.891%	$1,178	$174,037
660–679	4.105%	$1,209	$185,140
640–659	4.535%	$1,272	$207,890
620–639	5.081%	$1,354	$237,605

Source: FICO[27]

A credit report is a detailed report of your credit history that lists everything about your credit history, including personal data like where you live and where you have lived, your employment history, and your Social Security number. It provides a summary of your credit history and a detailed accounting. You're entitled to get a copy of your credit report for free once a year.

GETTING YOUR CREDIT SCORES AND CREDIT REPORT

You hear all the time about getting free credit reports and scores online, but if you've ever tried to get them, you might have run into a few roadblocks. While you're entitled to get your credit report for free once a year, you're not entitled to get a free credit score.

The best place to get your free credit report is directly from the Federal Trade Commission at AnnualCreditReport.com. You can also call them to obtain your free annual report at 1-877-322-8228. The law dictates that you can also get a free report from each of the three credit-reporting agencies: Transunion, Equifax, and Experian. Their websites will let you know how to obtain them, but you will most likely have to pay extra if you want to access them online (see Table 17).

TABLE 17

GET A FREE COPY OF YOUR CREDIT HISTORY OR REPORT FRAUD

Once a year you can contact the major credit bureaus to get a copy of your credit history for free. You can either apply online or over the phone. If your identity is ever stolen, you'll have to contact them as well.

AGENCY	WEBSITE	PHONE NUMBER	FRAUD HOTLINE
Equifax	www.equifax.com	1-800-685-1111	1-888-766-0008
Experian	www.experian.com	1-888-397-3742	1-888-397-3742
TransUnion	www.transunion.com	1-800-916-8800	1-800-680-7289

You might also want to get your credit score from time to time just to check it. There are a few sites where you can get a free credit score estimate like Credit.com, CreditKarma.com, CreditSesame.com, and Quizzle.com, but this isn't your official FICO score. You can get your official FICO score from FICO directly at myfico.com or from other sites.

BUILDING OR REPAIRING YOUR CREDIT SCORE

If you don't have a credit history or if you have a bad credit score, you'll want to start working on building a good credit score (see Table 18). Here are some key things that the Consumer Financial Protection Bureau suggests you do to build and maintain a good credit score:

Always Pay on Time   To maintain or build a great score, make sure you pay all your bills on time, including cell phone bills, medical bills, utility bills, parking tickets, and alimony or child support payments. If a collection agency ever contacts you, respond as soon as possible and offer to pay the amount in full immediately if they remove the notice of collections from your credit report. If you are going through financial difficulties and are having a hard time paying your bills, focus on paying whichever bills you can afford to pay in full or those that have been overdue the longest; that will limit the damage to your credit report.

Don't Max It Out   Since part of your credit score is calculated based on how much of your credit you are using, try not to max out your cards. In fact, experts suggest that you should never use more than 30% of your credit limit.

Start Early   The longer you've had a credit account, the better your score will be. If you don't have one already, make sure you get a credit card as soon as you can, start using it responsibly and paying off credit. Also, don't close old accounts if you have used them responsibly for years. Having longstanding accounts can help your score.

TABLE 18

SMART MOVES THAT WILL IMPROVE YOUR CREDIT

SMART MOVE	WHY
Getting a credit card	A credit card will help you establish a credit history. Open one sooner rather than later as the length of time you've had a credit account helps improve your credit score. Charge things on your card during the month and then pay it off after you get your statement.
Getting a department store credit card	Department store cards are seen as different from regular credit cards on your credit history, giving you more credit diversity on your report.
Keeping your balance below 30% of the credit available to you	This is the optimal amount and will give you extra points on your score.
Increasing your credit limit	When your credit limit increases, the proportion of credit you're using decreases and improves your score.
Getting a late payment removed	If you can get your lender to remove the late payment, this will reverse the bad mark on your credit.
Getting incorrect information removed	Getting incorrect info removed from your credit report will ensure that it won't penalize you.

Source: Consumer Financial Protection Bureau[28]

HOW TO PREVENT IDENTITY THEFT

Identity theft is one of the worst nonviolent crimes. When someone steals your identity, they haven't just stolen money—they've stolen it in your name. According to the Identity Theft Resource Center, if your identity is stolen it will take you an average of 600 hours to restore your good name.[29] That works out to three weeks and four days of working 24 hours—in other words, all your free time for the foreseeable future.

In 2012, more than 12.6 million people had their identities stolen.[30] It's far better to work a little harder now to protect your identity than to have to sit on hold with credit card companies and credit bureaus once it's already happened. Here are some tips to help prevent identity theft and protect your credit report and score.

Leave Your Social Security Card at Home This one is fairly easy. If your SSC is in your wallet, get up right now and take it out. Now you won't have to worry about your Social Security number leaking if someone steals your wallet.

Protect Your Mailbox If your mail is left in an unsecured box, be sure to collect it as soon as you can. If you notice you haven't received a monthly bill, call the company as soon as possible and cancel your account. Someone might have stolen your bill and might be using it to steal your identity.

Check Your Bills Check your bills for any transactions that aren't familiar. If you find one, report it to your credit card company immediately.

Buy a Shredder You need to use a shredder to destroy any papers, bills, credit card offers, or other documents that might have your personal information on them.

Protect Your Computer Protect any financial information you might have stored on your computer with antivirus software and strong passwords. Make sure to wipe your computer's hard drive clean if you sell it or give it away.

Ignore All Phishing Most phishing is pretty obvious, but criminals have stepped up their game. Even if you get an email that looks legitimate, never click the links but type the address in the browser yourself. If someone calls you and sounds legitimate, offer to call them back before handing over any personal data.

Get an Online Credit Card Some people get online credit cards with low credit limits to protect themselves in case their credit card details are stolen. Not only will the scammers not be able to charge a lot of purchases to your account, but you can also easily cancel your card. While shopping online, don't save your credit card information on any websites; it increases your chances of it getting stolen.

Freeze It If you're really concerned about identity theft, you can freeze your credit by calling each of the three major credit bureaus. You will most likely have to pay a small fee to freeze your credit, but it will prevent anyone from opening a new account in your name. If you want to unfreeze your credit, you will need to contact all the bureaus again and pay another fee to unfreeze it.

WHAT TO DO IF YOUR IDENTITY IS STOLEN

In case your identity is stolen, it's good to be prepared and know what you have to do to restore your good name. The most important thing you should do is keep a record of the process of restoring your credit. Buy a notebook and start writing down the names and titles of everyone you speak to and what they have told you.

Contact All Credit Providers Contact every company that you have a credit account with and let them know what has happened. Cancel your cards or lines of credit and have them reissued.

Contact Police Identity and credit card theft is a crime—report it. You might need to provide a police report to credit agencies. The police might also know of other similar criminal activity, and this can support your case.

Contact the Credit Agencies The next thing you should do is call one of the credit agencies and let them know what has happened. They will put a fraud alert on your credit accounts, which will stay on for 90 days, but you can renew it after it expires.

Create an Identity Theft Report Go to the Federal Trade Commission's website and fill out their online form for reporting fraud. Submit the form and save or print a copy. This will be your identity theft affidavit.

HOW IMPORTANT IS BUILDING CREDIT FOR MILLENNIALS?

Erin Lowry is the mastermind behind the popular blog *Broke Millennial*. She got her first credit card at 18 years old in order to start building credit and soon enough managed to build a stellar credit score. She shares what she learned along the way with you.

ON WHY OUR PARENTS AREN'T ALWAYS RIGHT "We innately look to our parents for guidance, and most of the time that's not a problem, but unfortunately a lot of Americans are not financially literate (or not literate on all fronts). I had a friend in college who was told by his mother that carrying a balance on his credit card was good for his credit score! His mom worked for a bank. You can't totally trust your parents on all money advice. You need to fact-check what they tell you because sometimes they're misinformed."

ON WHAT MILLENNIALS CAN DO TO IMPROVE THEIR CREDIT SCORES "The majority of Millennials have student loans, so they are already establishing credit. Getting a credit card can be a great way to add variety to your credit history. Because you're not paying back your student loans yet, you're not proving that you can pay back what you borrow. In college, it's really easy to get a credit card. The moment you graduate and you're not a college student, it's not as easy.

When you get your first credit card, you should be making a small purchase every month and paying it back. You need to show that you're using the credit and that you're trustworthy enough to pay it back. Still, you don't want to spend that much money with your first card because it will have a small credit limit and you want to use a small percentage of your credit limit."

ON WHAT MILLENNIALS DO TO HURT THEIR CREDIT SCORES

"Missing a single credit card payment can drop your score 100 points, especially if you have a high score. Some people think that if their bill is due on Thursday and they don't get paid until Friday, they're better off waiting until they can pay back their bill in full. You're better off paying the minimum on the day that it's due and paying off the balance the next day.

You also don't want to default on a loan, whether it's on a personal loan or a student loan. If you're having a hard time paying your student loans, you need to call your student loan servicer and let them know. If you call proactively, they are far more likely to help you then if you wait until something happens and you default on your student loan. A negative item on your credit report can stay there for seven years and that can really drag your credit score down.

Another way Millennials hurt their credit score is by not having any credit. I know that some people are hesitant to have a credit card because they're afraid it's going to lead to debt, but if you don't have a credit card, or a student loan, or a car payment, or a mortgage or some other way to establish credit history than that will make your life very expensive. Eventually, you will need to use credit and it will be more expensive for you to borrow."

ON WHY MILLENNIALS SHOULD CARE ABOUT THEIR CREDIT SCORE

"Having a strong credit score makes the rest of your financial life cheaper. If you have a strong credit score and you need a loan for any reason like a medical emergency, a house, or a car, then a strong credit score will equal lower interest on your loans, which will save you money. A poor credit score will mean higher interest on your loans, which will cost you more."

You want that strong credit score because you always want to be in the best situation if and when you have to borrow money.

CHAPTER

PERSONAL CREDIT

Unlike spending, repaying is a bit more complicated—not to mention difficult. Over the years, credit might have become your enemy, but it can also be a friend. In this chapter, we'll look at different forms of personal credit and how to use them.

KNOW YOUR TERMS

Have you ever felt like finance people use a different language? You go into a bank to apply for a loan, and all of a sudden they're throwing words at you that you know you're supposed to know but don't. The definitions below should help ensure you'll never be in that situation again.

Cosigner When a lender has any doubts about whether the person seeking a loan has sufficient income or a high-enough credit score, they will often make a request for a cosigner who has a higher credit score and sufficient income in order to issue the loan or provide a lower interest rate. By cosigning the loan, a cosigner pledges to pay the loan should the borrower default. Many private student loans require cosigners, but some have provisions allowing you to remove the cosigner from the loan after making a certain number of on-time payments.

Secured Secured credit tends to offer lower interest rates but for a reason. A secured credit account is one where you put up an asset you own as collateral. That means that if you fail to pay back the loan, the lender can seize the asset. Common types of secured credit include mortgages, car loans, and home equity lines of credit.

Unsecured An unsecured loan does not involve putting any assets up as collateral. These types of loans are riskier for the lender; because of this added risk, the lender will typically charge higher interest rates. Credit cards are the most well-known lines of unsecured credit.

Installment Loans An installment loan is a loan that you borrow and pay back over a certain amount of time. The installments are determined by an agreement between you and your loan issuer. Once you pay off your loan, the account is closed; during the course of paying off your loan, you cannot take out additional money.

Revolving Loans A revolving loan is one where you have been given a credit limit by your lender to use and pay back anytime you want, as often as you need. You generally have to pay a minimum toward any outstanding balances every month. A credit card is the most common form of revolving credit.

MAY I HAVE MORE CREDIT?

Kari Luckett, a Financial Expert and Content Strategist for *Compare-Cards*, has been able to keep her credit score high by asking every 6–12 months for an increase in her credit limit. Because part of your credit score calculates how much of your available credit you're using, increasing your credit limit will mean you're using a lower percentage of your total limit. According to Kari, "I have personally seen my own credit score grow by 100 points in 30 days, twice in one year, by simultaneously increasing my credit line and paying down a large amount of debt at the same time. Every 6 months, as long as you've managed your account responsibly and it remains in good standing, you can request a credit line increase and many times this can be done online by searching for a 'credit line increase' in your account. You may even have a pending offer waiting for you to accept."

APR This stands for annual percentage rate—the annual percentage you will be charged for borrowing funds.

Grace Period A period when you're not required to make payments.

Prime The prime rate is the rate given to the borrowers with the best credit scores. Most borrowers must pay a certain percentage above prime depending on their credit scores.

THE SKINNY ON YOUR CREDIT CHOICES

In the wide world of credit options, you have a lot of choices, but some are better than others (see Table 19). Here is a rundown on common forms of credit and how to best use them.

Credit Cards Credit cards are the most common form of credit. While most of us think we know a lot about them, not all use them correctly. Credit card debt is the worst debt to have because it generally carries a high-interest rate.

- **The Right Use:** The best use for a credit card is as a way to build your credit history and improve your credit score. Paying off your balance in full each month makes it easy to track your spending, and you can often earn travel rewards.

- **Finding the Right One:** There are three main things to consider when picking a credit card. The first is the interest rate. You want a card with a low interest rate. Anything under 14% is relatively low for credit cards.

The next thing you want to look at is what kinds of rewards the cards feature, including what rewards they offer to sign up. Make sure you choose a reward that is for something you'll actually use. Travel and cash-back cards are often the best since they tend to give the highest payouts.

Finally, you want to take the annual fee into account. If the annual fee is more than you can expect back in rewards, take that into account when you choose your card.

TABLE 19
WHERE TO LOOK ONLINE FOR THE BEST CREDIT DEALS

These sites compare different types of loans to help you choose the right one.

TYPES OF LOANS	WHERE TO LOOK
Credit Cards	CreditDonkey.com, CreditSesame.com, CardHub.com, CardRatings.com, NerdWallet.com, Bankrate.com
Mortgages	Bankrate.com, LendingTree.com, eLoan.com, Zillow.com
Loans	Bankrate.com, eLoan.com, LendingTree.com

Lines of Credit Lines of credit can either be secured or unsecured. Most secured lines of credit are home equity lines of credit and car equity lines of credit. Secured lines of credit generally have lower interest rates since there is less risk to the lender. See Table 20 for a comparison with credit cards.

- **The Right Use:** Lines of credit can be useful to pay for things that you might otherwise put on your credit card, to handle emergencies, to fund home repairs or improvements, to buy cars or pay for their repairs, or to consolidate other loans with higher interest rates. They're best used when they're helping you save money on interest or do things that will increase the value of your home.

- **Finding the Right One:** Shop around among banks and other issuers to find one that provides you with the lowest interest rate.

TABLE 20

HOW MUCH YOU SAVE BY CHOOSING THE RIGHT CREDIT FACILITY

This table shows you how much you would save in interest over one year by using a low interest line of credit to pay for something rather than a credit card. This calculation assumes you are not actively paying off this amount but carrying it on your card.

TYPE OF CREDIT	INITIAL AMOUNT	ESTIMATED INTEREST RATE	INTEREST	TOTAL
Credit Card	$5,000	13.02%	$651	$5,651
Credit Card	$5,000	18%	$900	$5,900
Line of Credit	$5,000	7%	$350	$5.350
Line of Credit	$5,000	4%	$200	$5,200

Personal Loans Personal loans can also be secured or unsecured, but they are installment loans and not revolving loans. You take out a specific amount, and you're given a specific amount of time to pay it back.

- **The Right Use:** These can often be used to pay for things like medical bills or other unexpected expenses, or to consolidate other loans.
- **Finding the Right One:** Shop around to find a loan that will offer you the lowest interest rate.

Borrowing from Friends or Family Sometimes emergencies happen, and your only option is to ask family or friends for help. While asking family and friends for help might seem like an easy and quick way to borrow money, it could affect your relationships.

- **The Right Use:** Only turn to family and friends when you truly have no other options. When you do borrow money from friends or family members, be sure to write up an agreement detailing the terms of the loan and when you will pay them back. Offer to pay them interest on the amount loaned, and pay them back in a timely manner.
- **Finding the Right One:** Only borrow from family or friends if they are willing and able to never see the money they lend to you again. Be sure it's for something you really need.

Payday Loans Payday loans are terrible and should be avoided at all costs. They charge an absurd amount of interest; while many states limit the APR that a payday lender can charge, where there aren't limits, it's not uncommon to see the APR of a 14-day loan work out to well above 500%.

NOT SO FAST! INTEREST-FREE 401(K) LOANS AREN'T AS GREAT AS THEY SEEM

Did you know that you could borrow interest-free from your 401(k)? It seems like a great idea. Instead of borrowing and paying interest, you can access your own savings. But taking money out of your 401(k) has a cost, and that's the interest that you would have been making on your investments had that money stayed there. While it might not seem like you're losing anything now because the returns would be coming in the future, it might make more sense to borrow money at a low interest rate than take it out of your investments. After all, you can expect to make around 7% to 8% per year if you're investing in the stock market.

THE PSYCHOLOGY OF DEBT

Going deeply into debt to buy things you don't need doesn't make rational sense. There are, however, complex psychological factors at play that explain why we might spend more than we can afford. A factor called hyperbolic discounting, for example, causes us to discount what will happen to us in the future and focus instead on what is happening right now. We thus focus on having fun in the present without considering the pain that we will feel when we're still paying that debt off in the future. Our sense of scarcity also kicks in to make us believe that the bike that we've fallen in love with will never go on sale again. That leads us to feel we must act now, even if saving up and paying in cash would be smarter.

WHAT YOU NEED TO KNOW ABOUT PERSONAL CREDIT

Grayson Bell, who runs Debt RoundUp.com, is no stranger to the world of personal credit. He has been giving people advice on how to use credit responsibly and get out of debt since 2012, when he finished paying off more than $50,000 in credit card debt that he acquired while he was in college. He has these great tips for you.

HE THINKS THAT MILLENNIALS NEED TO HEAR THIS ABOUT CREDIT "Don't be afraid of credit. A credit card and loans are just tools to help you achieve something. It's what you do with those products that will define your financial success. Credit is important in our society, and you can go far when you have quality credit and know how to use it."

ON REWARDS CREDIT CARDS "So many people love the idea of rewards credit cards, but they are only good if you plan on using the rewards and paying off your balance every month. No rewards card is good if you carry a balance. Rewards cards typically carry higher interest rates, so your rewards can be wiped out by one missed payment."

ON HOW TO USE CREDIT CARDS PROPERLY "You should only use credit cards for purchases you can actually afford. If you can pay cash for it, then you can use a credit card. The reason people get into trouble is because they borrow money from their credit card company and just keep paying the minimum payment. That's a recipe for disaster."

CHAPTER

STUDENT LOANS

When you're growing up, people always tell you that a great education is priceless. Well, anyone who has crossed a stage on graduation day with a diploma or degree in his or her hands knows that's not true. A great education carries a price: thousands of dollars in student loans. In this chapter, we'll look at scaling your mountain of student-loan debt.

STUDENT LOANS 101

Student loans are generally referred to as "good" debt. That's because they have a relatively low interest rate, and most studies have shown that the increased income that results from getting an education offsets the cost of the student loan. Unfortunately, this isn't always the case. Students are racking up more student-loan debt than they can afford to pay off. For these students, their debt is hardly "good" (see Figure 8 for how you stack up).

The first thing you need to know about student loans is that they don't die. They are the zombies of the credit world and will keep coming for you until you die or pay them off. Unlike all other types of loans, they cannot be discharged in bankruptcy. According to Edvisors, the average student-loan debt in America is $33,000.[31] That's a lot.

FIGURE 8

HOW DO YOU RANK?

How does your student loan debt stack up to the amount other Millennials took out? A survey of today's 27-year-olds who went to college reveals the following pattern of student loan debt:

TYPICAL STUDENT POPULATION BY LOAN AMOUNT TAKEN OUT

0$ — 39.8%

$1–$9,999 — 16.0%

$10,000–$24,999 — 20.2%

$25,000–49,999 — 13.1%

$50,000+ — 10.9%

Source: The Atlantic[32]

DOES THIS REPAYMENT PLAN MAKE ME LOOK BROKE?

You've graduated. Perhaps you've struggled to find work or are making less than you expected to be making. It doesn't matter, because six months after graduating it's time to start paying the piper: Your student loans are due. If you haven't already thought about it, give some consideration to choosing a student loan repayment plan. For federal loans, these are your options:

The Standard Plan Of all the student loan options, this plan will allow you to pay off your loan most quickly and pay the least amount of interest. It calculates your payments based on a ten-year term.

The Graduated Plan This plan starts out with lower monthly payments and gradually increases every two years. This can be helpful for those who don't make very much right after they graduate but expect their salaries to increase over time. You'll pay more interest overall since you'll be paying mostly interest in the first years of the plan; this plan is usually a ten-year plan.

WRITE A BREAKUP LETTER TO YOUR DEBT

Melanie Lockert, who started the blog *DearDebt.com*, had $81,000 in student loan debt when she graduated from NYU with her Master's degree. She believes that there is a significant emotional aspect to student-loan debt that people don't usually talk about. She started writing breakup letters to her debt and has encouraged others to do so as well: "*Dear Debt* aims to help borrowers by providing alternative advice on how to pay off debt, including . . . allowing people to express the emotional side of debt with 'dear debt letters,' or breakup letters to debt. I found that many people give advice but don't talk about the emotional aspects of debt. Debt is so isolating and full of guilt and shame. I wanted to create a platform to talk about it."

Income-Based or Pay-as-You-Earn Plans You're eligible for these plans if you owe more than you make in a year. These plans limit how much you pay to 10% or 15% of your monthly income, and take your family size into account. You will pay significantly more in interest with these plans, but after 20 to 25 years your loans might be forgiven (see Table 21). All is not lost!

TABLE 21

YOU CAN GET YOUR FEDERAL STUDENT LOANS FORGIVEN

According to Andy Josuweit of StudentLoanHero.com, there are more than seventy ways to get your student loans forgiven. Here are just a few of them.

LOAN FORGIVENESS PROGRAMS	HOW TO DO IT
Teach	If you have a Perkins Loan, you can get it partly forgiven if you teach in a school district that serves low-income families. The more years you teach, the more of your loan is forgiven.
Serve Your Country	If you join the military, you might qualify for a student-loan repayment program.
Work for the Government or a Nonprofit	If you make 120 qualifying payments while working for a qualified employer, you can get the remainder of your loans forgiven.
Wait 20 to 25 Years	Many income-based repayment programs will forgive the remaining balance on your student loans after 20 to 25 years of payments.
Be a Doctor or Nurse	If you agree to work in an under-served area, you can potentially qualify for student loan forgiveness programs.

Source: StudentLoanHero.com

Income-Contingent Plan With this plan you'll pay the lesser of either 20% of your discretionary income, or what you would pay on a fixed payment plan over a twelve-year term. This will require you to pay more than the income-based or pay-as-you-earn plans, but doesn't have an income requirement to enroll in it.

Income-Sensitive Plan Your payments on this plan will depend on your annual income and will change as your income changes. Payments for this payment plan last 10 years. Since the amount of the payments changes, you'll pay more upfront in interest than you would with a ten-year standard plan.

Extended Payment Plan You can make smaller payments over a longer period with this plan. To be eligible, you need to have more than $30,000 in student loans. You can make either fixed or graduated payments and extend your loan up to 25 years. See Table 22 for info on the relationship between interest paid and loan length.

TABLE 22
HOW MUCH MORE INTEREST WILL YOU PAY?

You can potentially extend the length of your repayment over a longer period of time than the typical ten years, but should you? This chart will show you how much more interest you will pay if you extend your repayment term based on borrowing $10,000 at a rate of 6.8%.

YEARS	MONTHLY PAYMENT	TOTAL AMOUNT PAID	TOTAL INTEREST PAID
5 Years	$197.07	$11,824.18	$1,824.18
10 Years	$115	$13,809.66	$3,809.66
15 Years	$88.77	$15,978.10	$5,978.10
20 Years	$76.33	$18,321.22	$8,321.22

Source: FICO[33]

WHAT ABOUT PRIVATE LOANS?

Like federal student loans, most private student loan providers have standard ten-year payment plans. They also often offer alternatives to extend your loan repayments to fifteen, twenty, or twenty-five years. While lower monthly payments can help if you're really tight on money, you will pay significantly more in interest over the life of your loan. Check with your lender to see what their options are and choose one that will allow you to comfortably pay off your loan the fastest.

ONE LOAN TO RULE THEM ALL: CONSOLIDATE YOUR LOANS

Most students graduate with a mix of private and federal student loans. By consolidating your loans, you can simplify things, lower your monthly payments, get a fixed rate, and get a lower interest rate.

While it can be helpful to consolidate your loans in order to lower your monthly payments, it might also mean you'll extend the life of your loan and end up paying more interest over its lifetime. Also, federal student loans need to be consolidated separately from private student loans if you want to keep the great terms that federal loans offer.

BREAK UP WITH YOUR PRIVATE LENDER AND SAVE

Guess what? You're not stuck with your student loan lender. You can refinance your student loans with another lender and potentially get a better interest rate and repayment terms—maybe even saving you thousands of dollars over the course of your loan.

If you took out private student loans when you were in your early 20s, you could probably only qualify for a relatively high-interest rate. If you've graduated and now have a job that pays you well and a higher credit score, try to get a better student loan deal.

You can save more money if you refinance sooner in your student loan term; there are a number of companies that specialize in student loan refinancing, like CommonBond, cuStudentLoans, SoFI, Citizens Bank, and Education Success Loans. See Table 23 for sites and apps that can help get your debt under control.

Be careful to read the fine print of your new student loan agreement. You don't want to give up the bells and whistles of your former plan like income-based repayment or the ability to defer your loan if you return to school or lose your job. Finally, before you make the switch, do the math; make sure that refinancing will actually save you money.

TABLE 23

WEBSITES AND APPS TO HELP TAME THAT DEBT

Whether your student-loan debt is as feisty as a lion or as tame as a tabby cat, these websites and apps will help you get it under control.

APP/WEBSITE	WHAT IT DOES
Tuition.io	Helps borrowers keep track of who holds their student loans, how much they still owe, and when their payments are due.
SponsorChange.org	This website helps charitable students pay down their student-loan debt. In exchange for volunteering at nonprofit organizations, SponsorChange.org helps match student loan borrowers with people who will contribute to paying off their student loans.
Student Loan Hero	Student Loan Hero helps you track your student loans and shows you how to save money on your payments. It helps you apply for income-based repayment programs, learn about loan forgiveness programs you might qualify for, and defer loans if you're facing hardship.

WHAT IF YOU CAN'T PAY?

You're living your life, and everything is going okay. You have a job, and you're making enough money to pay your student loan bills. But then something happens and you're struggling. What can you do if you can't pay? You have a few options.

Repayment Plan Change If you're struggling to make your monthly payments but can still afford to pay something, call your lender to negotiate a different payment plan. This can be a quick and easy solution to your problem. When things get better, you can always switch to another repayment plan. You can do so once a year.

Deferment A federal student loan deferment allows you to suspend your monthly payments, but only under very specific circumstances. If you're going to school, facing economic hardship, are unemployed, or serving in the military, you might qualify. For a Federal Perkins Loan, you can also get a special deferment for being a Peace Corps volunteer or a law enforcement officer.

If you have a subsidized federal student loan, the government will pay the interest for you while your loan is deferred. If not, the interest will accrue; when you start paying again, you will owe more than you previously owed. You can combat this by paying just the interest on your loans while they're in deferment.

Forbearance Forbearance is similar to deferment in that it gives you a temporary break on your student loans, but it doesn't have the added bonus of potentially having your interest paid. To qualify for forbearance, you need to be in one of the following situations: in poor health, completing a medical or dental internship or residency, in financial hardship, or having personal problems that you could not foresee.

You can also qualify if you're serving in AmeriCorps, teaching in a position that qualifies for the Teacher Loan Forgiveness Program, or serving in the military. Some private student loans have an option similar to forbearance as well.

Defaulting—the Thing to Never, Ever, Ever Do You're officially in student loan default when you haven't made a payment in 270 days, or nine months, and you haven't spoken to your lender about alternative options. Basically, those who default stick their heads in the sand and hope their student loans will go away. Unfortunately, the loans don't go away, but the lenders get new legal powers to make your life a living hell.

SAVE YOURSELF! TIPS TO MINIMIZE STUDENT DEBT

If you're currently a student or thinking about going back to school, you might wonder what you can do to keep from sinking into the student loan quicksand. Here are a few things you can do to avoid student-loan debt.

Find Scholarships Take advantage of scholarships whenever you can. If you focus on ones that you're perfectly suited for—or ones that will be less likely to get applicants—you can increase your chances of getting some of that free money.

Choose a Cheap College Unless you're going to one of the top twenty-five schools, it doesn't matter which institution's name is on your degree. Choose a school strategically. Find a school that has a good reputation but doesn't charge enormous tuition fees each year.

Live Like a Student Living large while you're a student isn't worth the painful years of struggling to pay off student loans if you're not careful. Eat frugally, keep your expenses low, and be as prudent as possible.

Pay Your Interest If you do need to take out student loans and they are private student loans or unsubsidized federal loans, then interest will accumulate while you're going to school. This will add thousands of dollars to your total debt, increase the amount of interest you pay over the course of your loan, increase the length of your loan, and increase your monthly payment. If you can pay the interest charges on your loans while you're in school, you'll pay less over the course of your loans and pay them off sooner.

WHAT DO I NEED TO KNOW ABOUT STUDENT LOAN DEBT?

After taking out more than $70,000 in student loan debt, Andy Josuweit's balance ballooned to more than $100,000 from spending the years after graduating either unemployed or underemployed. This experience—and the complications of managing sixteen different loans with three different service providers—led him to found *Student Loan Hero,* a service that helps borrowers organize, track, and pay back their student loans.

ON WHY IT'S SO DIFFICULT FOR MILLENNIALS TO PAY BACK THEIR LOANS "Many Millennials are unemployed or underemployed when they get out of school. Many have a tremendous amount of different loans, which are owned by different lenders and servicers. It's really confusing."

ON THE MOST IMPORTANT THING TO REMEMBER "It's a marathon, not a sprint. You're going to be paying off your student loans for a long time. You need to think about stopping the bleeding by either generating more income or entering into one of the federal student loan payment programs to avoid default. The worst situation is to default on your loans because you didn't apply for deferment or an income-based repayment plan. When this happens, 16% of the student loan is added to the principal as a default fee."

ON HOW TO KEEP MOTIVATED "Borrowers get mentally and emotionally frustrated, and it's important that they recognize that they're not alone; there are 42 million other student loan borrowers in the United States. The situation will work itself out so long as you keep pushing through it."

12

CHAPTER

BECOMING DEBT-FREE

N o one intends to rack up debt that they can't pay back, but life happens. No matter how you got into debt, you shouldn't feel ashamed of it. Shame isn't a productive emotion. If you spend all your energy feeling bad about having gotten yourself into the situation you're in, then you'll have less energy to put together a plan and get out of debt. You're not a bad person because you've racked up debt, and your situation isn't hopeless. There are ways to get out of this with your self-esteem and your credit rating intact. This chapter looks at strategies to do just that.

STOP DEBT IN ITS TRACKS

The first thing you need to do is stop going further into debt. While many people find themselves in debt because of life circumstances that are beyond their control, others simply develop bad habits and don't pay enough attention to their finances. No matter which camp you find yourself in, you need to stop accumulating debt. This might mean drastically reducing your expenses by moving to a cheaper apartment, selling your car, or cutting out all nonessentials from your budget. If there isn't a way to spend less, then it might mean getting a second job or starting a side hustle (see Table 24 and Chapter 4).

TABLE 24
CREATIVE OPTIONS FOR PAYING OFF DEBT FASTER

CREATIVE OPTION	WHY?
Get a side hustle	If you have a high-interest loan or credit card, one of the best ways to pay it off is to make more money and apply it to your debt.
Get a consolidating loan	If you have a home or own a car, you can use it as collateral for a low-interest loan to pay off your credit card debt. The lower interest rate will help you pay it off faster.
Transfer your balance	If you can get a credit card that offers 0% on balance transfers for at least one year, consider transferring your debt to that card. There are cases of people who keep transferring their debt to 0% interest cards until they pay it off. Just make sure to read the fine print.
Give up your savings	If you're making less than 1% on your savings account and paying more than 8% on your credit card debt, you're paying money for the luxury of having cash. While you should have a small cash reserve, some people sacrifice their savings to pay debt faster.

NEGOTIATE YOUR RATES

The next thing you need to do is call up all the companies you owe money to and try to negotiate a lower interest rate. Make sure you are speaking to a manager who has the power to lower your rates; politely tell them that another bank has offered you a lower rate and you would like to know if they can meet it. They might not be able to meet the lower rate, but they might be able to give you a break on what you're currently paying.

CONSOLIDATE YOUR DEBT

If you are in danger of bankruptcy, you might be able to go to a debt consolidation service. They can sometimes buy your debt at a discount and pass some of the savings to you through a lower interest rate. Be careful because some scammers pretend to be able to help you with your debt and just take your money. See Table 25 for more on potential consolidation benefits.

CREATE A REPAYMENT PLAN

Having a sense of how long you will have to work to pay off your debt can help motivate you. Create a countdown to stay on track; break up your journey into smaller milestones so that you have a chance to celebrate along the way. Paying off debt can be draining and tiresome if you feel like the end goal is too far in the future.

TABLE 25

HOW SMALL CHANGES IN YOUR INTEREST RATE MAKE A HUGE DIFFERENCE

Stacy Johnson from MoneyTalksNews.com shows how you can save a significant amount of money by consolidating high-interest debt under a lower interest rate, either through a balance transfer or a consolidation loan.

ORIGINAL DEBT AMOUNT	INTEREST RATE	MONTHLY PAYMENT	INTEREST PAID	YEARS TO PAY
$10,000	15%	$250	$4,000	5
$10,000	10%	$250	$2,215	4
$10,000	7.25%	$250	$1,482	4

Source: MoneyTalksNews.com[34]

DEBT-STACKING METHOD

The debt-stacking method involves "stacking" or ordering your loans or credit cards based on which is charging the highest interest rate. If you can't consolidate your accounts under a lower interest rate, this method suggests that you pay off the account with the highest interest rate first since that is the one that is costing you more interest on a monthly basis. Once that account is paid off, you would then start paying off the account with the second highest interest rate. Because you're always directing your money toward the account that is charging you the most in interest, you maximize every repayment. This method is the fastest method to get out of debt and the method that will ensure you pay the least interest overall.

DEBT-SNOWBALL METHOD

Some people don't agree that the debt-stacking method is the best way to get out of debt. According to them, the problem with the debt-stacking method is that it doesn't pay enough attention to the psychological motivation of the debtor.

Instead of choosing to pay off the credit card with the highest interest rate first, they believe you should choose to pay off the credit card with the lowest balance. By paying off the card with the lowest balance first, you get to experience a quick win. This win will help bolster your efforts and energize you to pay off the next smallest balance. This second quick win will help you continue to be motivated to pay off all subsequent balances.

As you pay off one balance after another, the amount that you were paying toward the minimum payments on those cards will work like a snowball and accelerate your repayment. While this method isn't as fast or as cost-effective as the debt-stacking method, you might find this method more effective if you have a hard time sticking to the debt-stacking method. See Table 26 for some apps to help keep you on track.

THE SEVEN-MONTH ITCH: KEEPING MOTIVATED

Paying off debt diligently can lead to a phenomenon called debt fatigue. You start to wonder if you'll ever get out of debt and if it will all be worth it in the end. You feel defeated and exhausted from having to always maintain your willpower. Here are some tips that will help you stay on track even when it gets difficult.

Get Friends to Hold You Accountable Tell your friends, your family, and your partner about your repayment journey and ask them to help keep you on track. If they know your situation, they might be less likely

TABLE 26

THE BEST DEBT REPAYMENT APPS

APP	WHY
Ready for Zero	You link all your debts to your account, and it will create a personal repayment plan for you and keep you motivated along the way.
Debt Free	Debt Free uses the debt-snowball method and will help you focus on eliminating debt in one account at a time.
Debt Payoff Pro	This app also focuses on the debt-snowball method and has great reports showing your total debt amount and your progress.
iQuick Debt Payoff	Uses the debt-stacking method to help you pay off loans faster and pay the least amount of interest.

to suggest you do things that will cost a lot of money. If your friends have debt too (see Figure 9), consider competing with one another to see who can put the largest proportion of their income toward paying off their debt each month or who can pay off their debt more quickly.

Don't Deprive Yourself If you keep telling yourself you can't have the latte when that's all you can think about all day, you're going to wear yourself out and be miserable. Find a way to fit the most important luxuries into your budget. Maybe you get a latte once or twice a week, or you cut back on other things to allow yourself that small treat.

Set Up Small Rewards Paying off debt can be a long slog, and that can make it psychologically difficult to motivate yourself to stick to your repayment plan. If you can't see the light at the end of the tunnel, you might be less likely to make the sacrifices that you need to make now so that you can reach that beautiful debt-free future. That's why you need to set up smaller goals to celebrate as you pay off debt and give yourself

FIGURE 9

SINKING IN CREDIT CARD DEBT?
YOU'RE NOT ALONE

According to Consumer Reports, a third of Americans don't own a credit card. Of those that do, **46%** carry their balances over:

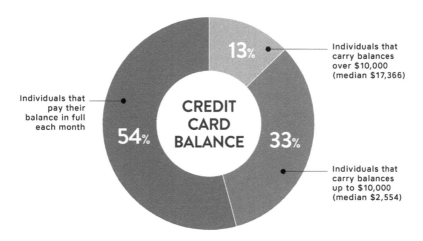

Individuals that carry balances over $10,000 (median $17,366)

Individuals that pay their balance in full each month

CREDIT CARD BALANCE

Individuals that carry balances up to $10,000 (median $2,554)

Source: Consumer Reports[35]

corresponding rewards. If you can find a way to feel a sense of accomplishment and to have a little fun while you're in the middle of the long slog of debt repayment, you'll be more likely to keep at it and reach your goal.

Adjust Your Goals If you're having a hard time sticking to your repayment schedule or if you're feeling overwhelmed by debt fatigue, you might consider adjusting your repayment schedule to be more reasonable. You shouldn't make yourself completely miserable in order to pay off your debt. While paying off debt faster is generally better, that is no longer true if you lose your ability to enjoy life.

Make Plans Planning for your debt-free future can help you keep your eye on the prize and get you over the fatigue. Plan to do some exciting things that you've always wanted to do but couldn't because you were paying off your debt.

THE PSYCHOLOGY OF PAYING OFF DEBT

Getting into debt is not always a rational process, and for that reason the best way to get out of debt is not always that most rational either. Rationally, the debt-stacking method is the best choice for paying off debt since you will pay it off faster and save money in interest, but research shows that the debt-snowball method is actually more effective. A study by Kellogg School of Management found that people who used the debt-snowball approach increased their likelihood of getting out of debt. The problem with paying down the balances with the highest interest rates first is that sometimes those are the biggest balances, and you don't feel like you're making as much progress when you focus on those first. That lack of progress makes people get discouraged and give up.

NEVER AGAIN! MAKE A VOW TO STAY DEBT-FREE

If you've struggled to repay your debt, you probably don't want to go into debt again anytime soon. What can you do to avoid it? Once you've gotten out of debt, make a pledge to yourself to never go back. Consider continuing to live frugally and devoting a portion of your income toward savings that will help cushion you in case something unexpected and costly happens. While you shouldn't avoid credit, learn how to use it responsibly.

WHAT CAN I DO TO PAY OFF DEBT OR STOP MY DEBT FROM GETTING WORSE?

John Schmoll Jr. hasn't always made wise financial decisions, but he's doing pretty well these days. John now runs the personal finance blog *Frugal Rules*, but when he graduated college he had more than $25,000 in debt. Here's how he paid it off.

ON HOW HE GOT OUT OF DEBT "That's an easy one to answer—through a lot of hard work. Seriously, though, I did what I could to make extra money. Of course, that included my job, but it also meant taking on side hustles and selling things I wasn't using just to get extra money to throw at my debt. Ultimately, it was meeting with a debt consolidation company that really was a turning point for me. They introduced me to budgeting and tracking my spending—both of which I had never really heard of before. Without that I don't know that I would've paid off my debt. In total, it took close to six years to pay everything off."

HIS ADVICE TO MILLENNIALS ON GETTING OUT OF DEBT "For me, it was attaching a purpose to paying off the debt. We're goal-driven by nature, and setting it as a goal can be a great way to make solid progress. Beyond that, your attitude is going to be a huge part of paying off the debt. It's easy to focus on how debt happened or beat yourself up for it. Don't. Focus instead on what your debt-free life will be like. Use the time to teach yourself about ways to improve financially so you can hit the ground running in growing your wealth once the debt is gone. Lastly, give yourself an outlet. It can be easy to allow debt and its repayment to consume your life. An outlet will help you avoid debt fatigue."

ON STRATEGIES TO PAY OFF DEBT FASTER "Side hustle like there's no tomorrow. Find any way you can to make more money on the side. All of that money can be thrown at your debt, which will only speed up the repayment process."

ON WHAT MILLENNIALS SHOULD DO TO STOP SLIDING FURTHER INTO DEBT "I would recommend two things. The first is to track your spending. Everyone says that, but there is a reason behind it: it works! If you don't know where every dime is going, you're only going to make debt repayment take forever. It doesn't have to be difficult or tedious—you can go as old school as pen and paper, or a simple spreadsheet. The other is to determine your triggers. For me it was going out shopping with no purpose in mind, especially when I was unhappy about something. If I did that, it was much more likely I would spend money I did not have. Determine what your triggers are so you can catch those times where you may be justifying spending money you shouldn't be."

ON CREDIT MISTAKES MILLENNIALS SHOULD BE WARY OF "First, and most importantly, is to not view it as play money. Easy, but very important. Beyond that, my biggest recommendation is to view it as your own money. If you don't have enough cash on you to buy something that's $100 then you obviously couldn't buy it. View credit cards the same way. If you don't have the money, or don't know where it'll come from then don't use the card."

ON HACKS FOR GETTING OUT OF DEBT "Beyond finding ways to make more money find whatever motivates you and put up a picture of it. That allows you to have a daily reminder of the 'why' behind all of your work. That can keep you going in days you want to give up. Another thing I did was assign certain jobs to a specific debt. That mental accounting was a huge help to me as I knew exactly where that extra money was going and thus kept me on track."

HACKS

GET A CREDIT CARD THAT TELLS YOU YOUR CREDIT SCORE

One easy way to stay on top of your credit score is to get a credit card that sends you your score with your monthly bill. Erin Lowry from the blog *Broke Millennial* has a Discover card for exactly this purpose and suggests it as a way for other Millennials to monitor their credit as they try to rebuild it. Other cards provide you with the same information, such as the Barclaycard and the First Bankcard. Compare the cards and find the one that's right for you. Just make sure the credit score they're offering is the one you want.

STRATEGICALLY PAY DEBT TO IMPROVE CREDIT SCORE

While you can, follow the debt-snowball or the debt-stacking method to pay off your credit card debt. If you're focused on simultaneously improving your credit score, you might be better off getting your credit utilization to 20% to 30% of each card. Rather than focusing on one card and paying it off completely, focus on cards that you can get to 20% to 30% credit utilization. That way you'll achieve a better rating on all of your accounts.

KNOW THE STATUTE OF LIMITATIONS ON YOUR DEBT

Did you know that your debt has an expiration date? If you have not paid by that date, then your debt cannot be collected. While certain forms of debt are exempt, like student loans and mortgages, credit card debt has a statute of limitations. The timeline varies state by state. The clock starts when you put the last charge on your account. Be careful if you've almost reached the statute not to do anything that might restart the clock, like making a payment or another charge. Also, just because your debt has expired that doesn't mean that collectors will stop calling you or that it will be taken off your credit history. Creditors will continue to try to get you to pay, and could even still sue you. If the time has run out, however, you don't need to pay and they can't win their suit.

BEWARE OF CREDIT-REPAIR AGENCIES

If a company told you that they could repair your credit for a fee, would you pay it to them? Many people pay credit-repair agencies to help them clean up their credit because they're desperate to get a loan or a mortgage. The truth of the matter is that these companies often can't do much that you can't do yourself. You're entitled to dispute any inaccurate or unverifiable information on your credit report, and the credit bureaus must remove it after thirty days if they cannot find proof for it. Credit-repair companies are simply doing the work of writing to credit bureaus for you, something that you could easily do yourself. Many credit-repair agencies are run by scammers, so watch out for anyone who is promising that they can do something other than contacting credit bureaus for you. They are probably trying to take advantage of you.

MAKE BIWEEKLY PAYMENTS

Making biweekly payments on a loan or a mortgage could save you thousands over the course of a loan. By making your payments biweekly instead of monthly you end up making 26 payments each year, which is the equivalent to 13 monthly payments. In addition, the bank will sometimes apply your payments to your loan right away, thus saving you interest. If this plan interests you, make sure that there will actually be savings with your loan. Sometimes banks will make you pay to participate in this plan, in which case it makes more sense for you to just make an extra monthly payment. In others, they don't calculate interest biweekly, so sending in your payment won't impact how much you owe in interest.

CALCULATE YOUR DAILY INTEREST

One of the things that Melanie Lockert, founder of the blog *Dear Debt*, suggests is to calculate your daily interest rate. What does she mean by that? To get the daily interest rate on your student loans, for example, you can simply look at your student loan statements and calculate how much interest you're paying each month and then divide it by the number of days in that month. The number you get will represent how much you will be paying each day in interest. When Melanie first did her calculations, she was paying $11 per day just in interest fees; that served to help motivate her to pay off her debt.

THINKING DEBT IS INEVITABLE IS A SELF-FULFILLING PROPHECY

Sarah from *When Life Gives You Lemons, Add Vodka* suggests that believing that debt is inevitable leads to debt actually becoming inevitable. According to Sarah, "There are too many Millennials that believe debt is a given, and it's not. Stop assuming you'll always be in debt! If you think that way, it will become a self-fulfilling prophecy. You don't need to take out student loans to go to school." By believing that you can't escape student loans, you're less likely to look for alternatives and less likely to work hard to avoid them.

GET OVER YOUR STUDENT-LOAN CREDIT ANXIETY

According to Kari Luckett, Credit Expert and Content Strategist for *CompareCards*, Millennials with high student loans are scared to take out any more debt so they aren't using their credit cards. That will hurt them in the long run, and so she offers this advice:

"Don't be afraid to use your credit card daily. Millennials should be putting all purchases they already make on a daily basis on their credit card and then turn around and pay them off. Even if you pay it off within an hour of your charge, it still shows lenders that you're responsible and manage your account well."

GRADUATE STUDENT LOANS

If you're thinking about going to graduate school, you should know that you're eligible for more money. In fact, in 2014 you could take out up to $20,500 in Stafford Loans a year, and you're also eligible for Graduate PLUS Loans. Perkins Loans are available for students who meet certain criteria as well. Graduate student loans are somewhat different in that there are no subsidized graduate student loans, meaning interest will accrue on all your loans while you're in school. Just make sure before you decide to take out graduate student loans that you calculate that the debt that you'll incur will be offset by the increase you'll see in your earning capacity. If not, it might not make sense for you to go back to get a graduate degree.

TAKE COSIGNERS OFF YOUR STUDENT LOANS

If you had to get cosigners to help you qualify for private student loans, there is a way to get them taken off after the fact. While it varies, depending on which company issued your student loans, after you've made a certain number of on-time payments on your student loan (usually 12 to 24), you can send a letter asking that the cosigner be removed. This protects your cosigner from having their credit score jeopardized, or from having to pay your loans if you run into financial difficulties in the future.

STUDENT-LOAN SCAMS

Scams generally try to take advantage of desperate people; with the high levels of student-loan debt, many students are desperate to find ways to alleviate it. Some popular scams include asking for an upfront fee to help a borrower get the best interest rate for refinancing or consolidating your loan. Other popular scams prey on the difficulty of finding private student loans without a cosigner, or on the mistaken belief that a company can help you get your student-loan debt discharged. Never pay anyone a fee upfront, and never give out your personal information to any company that you don't recognize.

HOW TO DISPUTE CHARGES LIKE A PRO

If there is a charge you don't recognize on your account, you need to call your credit card company as soon as possible. If it is a charge that has been made fraudulently, the card will need to be cancelled and you will have to have the credit card company take that charge off your bill. If a company has charged you incorrectly or if you have bought a product that was poor quality, you can also call your company and put that charge on hold. Once it's on hold, you'll then need to try to resolve the issue with the merchant. If they don't respond to your request, you might have to put your complaint in writing and have the credit card company contact the merchant to get their side of the story and decide whether to allow the charge or not.

USE YOUR CREDIT CARD BENEFITS

Credit cards, especially premium or travel rewards cards, often come with benefits that few consumers know about and use. You're probably familiar with your rewards points, but do you know if your credit card offers things like trip-cancellation insurance, emergency health insurance while travelling out of the country, or rental car insurance? In addition, many credit card companies give you an extended warranty for up to one year on all products bought with your card, some give you return protection, and some even offer a best-value guarantee, which will refund you up to $250 if you find something you already bought advertised for less. Read your credit card booklet to be sure that you understand and use all the credit card perks available.

MINIMIZE YOUR CREDIT CARD FEES

What credit card companies will never tell you is that if you call them up to complain about certain fees, they are likely to waive them or give you a discount. You can also potentially get out of paying annual fees. If you sign up for a card with an annual fee, consider calling the credit issuer and asking that they waive the fee for the first year. When it comes time to renew your card, request that your annual fee be waived again. You can also call up the card issuer at any time and threaten to cancel your card if they don't waive the fee. While you won't always be successful, many times credit card companies will do what they can to keep you as a customer.

NEGOTIATE YOUR APR

The people who get things in this world are the ones that ask for them. While credit card companies often offer discounts on APR to lure new card holders, you can often get better rates by calling and negotiating. Your credit card company will never call a loyal customer and offer them a discount. You need to take the initiative to call them. Tell them that you're thinking about transferring your balance or cancelling the card; that will most likely motivate them to take action and make you an offer.

HOW TO PREVENT REPOSSESSION

Beyond paying what you owe, one of the easiest short-term ways to prevent repossession is to keep your car in your garage. If they can't get to it, then they can't take it away. You can also try to negotiate with your lender and pay a portion of what you owe or see if you can get an extension. If none of that works and your car gets taken, you can try to buy it back when it's put up for auction.

WHAT TO DO ABOUT DEBT COLLECTORS

If you're contacted by a debt collector, be sure to know your rights and what they legally can or can't do. There have been many reports of debt collectors taking advantage of consumers who don't know their rights by making threats that they can't legally follow through on. Consumers are protected from debt collectors by the Fair Debt Collection Practices Act and can make complaints against collectors who don't follow it.

The first thing you want to do is record calls with your debt collector. Tell them that you intend to record the conversation for your records and they might be on better behavior because of this. Don't provide the debt collector with any information that you don't need to provide them. They will ask you a lot of questions, but you should insist that all requests be made in writing. They are trying to figure out how much you will be able to afford to pay in the form of a settlement.

According to Gerri Detweiler from Credit.com, you can ask the debt collector at any given time who owns your debt, and they are obliged to answer you.[36] If your debt has been sold to a collections agency, you can often get off with a better settlement since they will have purchased the debt for pennies on the dollar. Collectors will often offer you a settlement and say that you have a limited amount of time in which to accept it. You can make a counteroffer based on what you can afford to pay; you can also dispute the debt or wait for a better offer. Make sure that whatever deal you make with a collector, it includes a provision that will keep the information off your credit report.

No matter what they might tell you, they cannot tell other people about your debts in order to shame you, with the exception of your spouse or your cosigner. By knowing how to deal with debt collectors, you're less likely to get manipulated by them.

PAY YOUR BILL MORE OFTEN

If don't have a lot of credit or if you plan on making a big purchase during the month, consider paying down your credit cards more than just once that month. As explained in the credit score section, your score is higher when you're only using about 30% of your total available credit and your available credit on each card. If you plan on putting more than that on your credit card in any one month, pay off all or part of that charge as soon as possible to ensure that you don't go above the 30% usage cutoff by the time your bill comes.

PHOTOSHOP YOUR CREDIT

I'm always amazed when I see the non-Photoshopped versions of celebrity cover photos. They just look so different. Imagine if you could Photoshop your credit and take out all the wrinkles and blemishes. Well, you can. If you make a late payment, you can call up your lender and have them remove the late payment from your credit report. First, you can ask for them to make a goodwill adjustment, which creditors will sometimes do if you have a good prior history of paying on time. In order to qualify for this, you might need to send them a letter requesting forgiveness. If that doesn't work, you could also offer to set up automatic payments if they erase the late payment from your credit history. Many lenders will be willing to do so.

MILITARY SERVICE MEMBERS AND DEBT

If you're on active duty in the military, you should know about the special credit-related rights and protections available to you. For example, because of the Soldiers and Sailors Civil Relief Act, you are eligible for a 6% rate of interest on loans you took out prior to assuming your active duty placement. That means that the 19% APR credit card that you are carrying a balance on and any other loans, including car loans, student loans, and mortgages, can magically be changed to 6%. All you have to do is send a request in writing with a copy of your military orders. You have up to 180 days after you are released from active duty to make the request. This law also protects you and your family from evictions for nonpayment of rent unless there is a court order. In addition, creditors cannot repossess your property while you are serving, which includes repossessing your car or foreclosing on your home.

THE AUTHORIZED USER SCORE HACK

If you have a close family member, such as a spouse, a parent, or a grandparent, who has good credit, there is a way you can get their good credit to work its magic on your credit score. This works most effectively if they have had a credit line for a long time that they've always paid on time and has a low balance compared to the credit limit. You just need to get them to add you as an authorized user on that credit card. They will get a card in your name, which they can then choose to actually pass on to you or not. This account will be added to your credit score and potentially give it a substantial positive boost. This is particularly helpful for establishing credit because it will add an account that has a long history of being paid on time—which you will get extra points for.

LEARN TO PRIORITIZE

If you're having a hard time paying your bills, be strategic and pay the bills that are reported on your credit report before paying anything else. These bills will ensure that once you weather your financial storm, you won't have such a long road ahead to repair your credit.

GET A CREDIT CARD WITHOUT AN INCOME OR A CREDIT SCORE

One way to get a credit card without income or a credit score is to get a secured card. This is different from a pre-paid credit card in that you provide cash collateral to open the account rather than paying the balance ahead of time. If you use this card responsibly for a period of time, this will build your credit, potentially increasing your credit line once you've developed a credit history.

Many people suggest that you get a pre-paid card in order to build your credit, but be careful if you choose this strategy. Not all pre-paid cards report your credit to credit bureaus. If they do not, that card will have no impact on your credit or your ability to get another card in the future.

TRAVEL REWARDS HACKING

Take advantage of the bonuses given by travel rewards cards when you sign up for them by timing when you sign up for a new card with a major purchase. For example, some cards might give you a free flight if you charge anywhere from $2,000 to $5,000 in the first few months of owning a card. If you know you're buying something expensive like a car or electronics or you're paying a bill like the lump sum cost of your car insurance or your taxes, then sign up for the card right before this and use the card to gain points.

Other travel hackers find ways to exploit the loopholes in the rules of the rewards programs set up by airlines, hotels, and credit card companies by charging money without actually spending it. They come up with strategies like sending people money online who they know and trust to return the money, buying coins, and buying gift cards. While some people think this falls into an ethical gray area, those that do it believe they are acting in good faith and in accordance with their cards' policies.

USE A WEBSITE TO KEEP TRACK OF YOUR REWARDS

Make the most of your credit card travel rewards by keeping track of them using a site like AwardWallet.com. AwardWallet.com helps you track your credit cards' travel rewards and also travel rewards offered by hotels, airlines, and other providers. You set up your accounts, and it tracks your points for you, even sending you alerts if your points are about to expire.

FIGURE OUT THE COST OF BORROWING

Borrowing money might seem like an easy solution, but we don't always realize how much we're actually spending when we buy something with borrowed money. To help you stop borrowing and be more careful with money that has been borrowed, it is useful to do a calculation of how much the borrowed money will actually cost you. Let's say you buy a laptop for $1,000 on your credit card. If it

takes you one year to pay it back and you have an interest rate of 18% APR, then that laptop will actually cost you $1,097. If it takes you two years, then it will cost $1,198. If you keep in mind how much more you'll be paying in interest, you'll be less likely to buy with credit.

ENROLL IN AUTOMATIC PAYMENTS

If you automate your payments, you'll be less likely to miss a payment and damage your credit score or have to pay late fees. Your lenders also might give you some perks and benefits for automatically paying your bills. Some student loan lenders offer a discount on your interest rate if you enroll in automatic payments. That discount can be as much as 0.25%, which can save you a significant amount of money in the long term. Just remember to check your bill every month to make sure that they are charging you the right rates and that there aren't any charges on your credit card that aren't yours.

BORROW FROM YOUR PEERS

Walk up to a stranger on the street and ask them to lend you money and you'll probably get the cold shoulder, but lending to strangers is the new rage. Websites like Prosper.com and LendingClub.com allow individuals you don't know to lend you money. These sites are great alternatives to traditional institutions and can be good for people who would have a hard time accessing funds otherwise. By borrowing from peer-to-peer (P2P) lending sites, you'll pay a lower interest rate, you won't have to wait so long to get approved, it will be easier to apply, and you're more likely to be funded.

While many P2P lending sites deal with strangers lending to strangers, sites like National Family Mortgage actually allow you to borrow money from your friends or relatives to buy a house, with the site facilitating the mortgage and managing the repayment process.

USE AN APP TO TRACK MONEY YOU LEND

If you're the friend who is always lending people $10 or $20, it can be difficult to keep track of who has paid you back. Apps like PayMeBack and SpotMe allow you to track things like how much people owe you and when they've paid you back. These apps make it easier to track and get your money back when you lend people larger amounts, or for roommates to track and share expenses.

PART

SAVING IT

13

DISPOSABLE INCOME

We all need to pay for necessities such as living expenses, utilities, food, transportation, health care, and taxes. After all your needs are taken care of, however, you are free to spend or save your income as you please. While it might be tempting to take whatever's left over and "make it rain" in your living room, there might be wiser ways to use your disposable income.

DO YOU WANT TO BE A MILLIONAIRE OR JUST LIVE LIKE ONE?

Why is it called disposable income, you might ask. It's because you are the master of this part of your paycheck's destiny. It is at your disposal to spend or save.

How much of your disposable income you allocate toward having fun now and how much you allocate to planning for a great future is an intensely personal decision. Many personal finance experts will tell you to live on the bare minimum and save as much money as you can for your future. While this is a great strategy for finding security, taking advantage of compound interest (see Figure 10), and ensuring that you have lots of money when you retire, it's not the best strategy for everyone.

FIGURE 10

WHY COMPOUND INTEREST IS AWESOME

Think about the money in your wallet right now. How much do you think one dollar bill will be worth by the time you retire? In the table on the right you can see how much a dollar will be worth when you retire, depending on when you first saved it and based on a 7% average annual rate of return.

AGE 1ST $ SAVED	VALUE AT AGE 65
20	$21.00
25	$14.97
30	$10.68
35	$7.61
40	$5.43
45	$3.87
50	$2.67
55	$1.97
60	$1.40

VALUE AT AGE 65 OF $1 SAVED, BY AGE FIRST SAVED

| $21 | $14.97 | $10.68 | $7.61 | $5.43 | $3.87 | $2.67 | $1.97 | $1.40 |
| AGE 20 | AGE 25 | AGE 30 | AGE 35 | AGE 40 | AGE 45 | AGE 50 | AGE 55 | AGE 60 |

Rather than give advice to all of you as though you're all the same person with the same values and dreams, let's look at the population as two groups: Millennials who spend more money today as saving hares and Millennials who save more money for tomorrow as frugal tortoises.

Are You a Saving Hare? Saving hares see money as a means to have fun and access experiences that add meaning and happiness to their lives.

Many of them put money away for the future, but they keep a sizable chunk of their disposable income to pay for pleasures that they want to experience now. Because they're so actively engaged in enjoying what their money can buy them in the present, they will likely cross the retirement finish line after the tortoises who diligently plod along the road to retirement. For the savings hares, this isn't necessarily a bad thing. Many are willing to work longer in the jobs that they have in order to do the things that they enjoy during their personal time. They often couldn't imagine living the life of the frugal tortoise because they see it as a life filled with painful sacrifices for a distant future. Saving hares want more balance when it comes to spending their disposable incomes.

Are You a Frugal Tortoise? Tortoises are motivated by the challenge of reaching important financial milestones and the freedom and security they expect to feel when they have achieved their goals.

While they often sacrifice their current wants or their time to achieve something in the future, they keep their eyes on the prize that motivates them; they don't necessarily feel that the sacrifices they are making are difficult. In fact, many like challenging themselves to be more frugal and enjoy both the process of saving money and the results. Many frugal tortoises take pleasure in the opportunity to use their creativity and ingenuity to help them get by with less. Ultimately, they want the freedom to not have to work, and the security to not have to worry about money. Of course, being overly frugal can be taxing in its own way.

Which Is Better? Hares and tortoises don't share a retirement plan. The frugal tortoise will have more safety and security with less risk. If something bad happens, they are better able to recover. In contrast, some saving hares don't save enough to achieve their goals, and can run into

FRUGAL BURNOUT

Frugal burnout is a real thing. If you're a frugal person, you can scrimp, save, and deny yourself things that you want for years in order to meet a savings goal that you've set up for yourself. That can be exhausting, making you feel demoralized and worn out. If you find yourself experiencing frugal burnout, first make sure that the goal you set was realistic. If it was not, adjust it. You're not a savings automaton and you have needs. Next, prioritize being more frugal in areas that provide you with the best return. Sometimes we wear ourselves out doing frugal things that are time-consuming and don't actually save a lot of money. Finally, figure out what you wish you had most, and cut back in areas that aren't as important to you.

trouble when they lose a job or get sick. There is a lot more risk in being a saving hare. Still, each of us needs to make the choices that are right for them. There is much more to life than how much is in your bank account when you die.

Not everyone necessarily fits into the tortoise or hare roles. Many people sit somewhere in the middle, or can easily display a combination of tortoise and hare qualities. This ability to balance the pros and cons of both sides can be incredibly beneficial. See Table 27 for tips for tortoises and hares.

ALLOCATING YOUR DISPOSABLE INCOME

I didn't just tell you about savings hares and frugal tortoises because I wanted to talk about bunnies and turtles. Depending on what camp you're in, you might allocate your money differently. Here are the steps and two sample allocations for both tortoises and hares.

TABLE 27

TOP TIPS FOR HARES AND TORTOISES

TIPS FOR HARES	TIPS FOR TORTOISES
You like to spend, so make sure you can't access your savings. Automatically put money into your savings or investment accounts every month, and be careful using credit cards.	If your budget is too restrictive, either save a little less or get a side hustle to make more money.
Make sure you have a financial plan so that you know how much you'll need to contribute toward your future and how much you can spend.	Make sure you're utilizing the money you save effectively. If it's sitting in a savings account, invest it.
Prioritize your spending so that every dollar you spend gives you as much pleasure as possible. Don't spend on things that are convenient.	Don't miss out on something that you'll regret later just because you don't want to spend money. Live and enjoy your life while you're saving.

Calculate Your Disposable Income How much of your budget is really disposable? Go through your budget to add up all the money that you choose every month how to spend. This is where you truly have a choice about what to do with that money.

Decide If You Want to Change the Allocation What will truly give you the most pleasure to spend your money on? It might be to invest it or it might be to go on a ski trip. If you're not saving enough, you might want to add more to your savings.

Automate Your Savings If you're a saving hare, the easiest way to ensure that you're saving what you need to save for your future is to automate your finances or pay yourself first. Don't even let yourself get your greedy little hands on money that is intended to be saved. By outsmarting yourself in this manner, you'll be less likely to overspend.

ULTIMATELY, HOW YOU CHOOSE TO USE YOUR DISPOSABLE INCOME COMES DOWN TO WHAT YOU VALUE MORE

How you allocate your disposable income depends on a number of factors, including how much you make. The more money you make, the more likely it is you will allocate a higher percentage to savings. Here are some sample allocations.

Sample Tortoise Allocation

- Fixed Monthly Costs: 30% to 40%
- Disposable Monthly Costs: 20% to 30%
- Savings: 30% to 50%

Sample Hare Allocation

- Fixed Monthly Costs: 40% to 45%
- Disposable Monthly Costs: 35% to 40%
- Savings: 15% to 25%

WHAT SHOULD I DO WITH MY DISPOSABLE INCOME?

Figuring out how to allocate your disposable income can be difficult; it can be useful to get advice from an expert. Sarah from the personal finance blog *When Life Gives You Lemons, Add Vodka* is one such expert. With a background in business administration, she started her blog in 2010 when she was a student and focused primarily on frugality, but as she's moved into the working world and made more money, the blog has shifted toward saving, investing, and building careers.

HOW SHOULD MILLENNIALS DECIDE HOW TO ALLOCATE THEIR DISPOSABLE INCOME? "There are quite a few factors that would have to be considered when looking at income allocation for Millennials, including where they live, financial responsibilities, and whether the Millennial is in debt. If they have debt, then other than a small entertainment budget, disposable income should be spent paying debt. Once any outstanding debts are gone, then they should be striving for at least a 50% savings rate."

WHY SHOULD YOU ALLOCATE YOUR DISPOSABLE INCOME TO SAVINGS? "It is important to have a balance between spending and saving disposable income; for people just starting out with saving, start small. It's unsustainable to suddenly start trying to save 50% of your income or put all of your disposable income into savings.

Here's a three-pronged approach to saving:

1. Save up a small emergency fund (about three months of your income) into a high-interest savings account that is highly accessible.

2. After the emergency fund is fully funded, begin saving for a future goal (home ownership, further education, whatever the case may be) in a short- to mid-term investment account. Starting with some sort of investment (whatever you are comfortable with) will help your money grow and help you learn about investing. Keeping money in a savings account instead of investing it is passing up the opportunity for compound interest.

3. Put a portion of your disposable income into a retirement savings account.

Having an emergency fund, savings for a future purchase or goal, and retirement savings is an efficient way to cover the short term and long term and cover you in the case of any emergencies."

WHY IT'S IMPORTANT TO HAVE FUN WITH YOUR MONEY "Extreme frugality to the point of not having fun with your money is unsustainable. Deprivation leads to excess; if you cut your budget back all the way and leave no room for fun, you'll end up exhausted and demotivated from such a restrictive budget and probably spending emotionally. It's all about balance!"

WHY IT'S IMPORTANT TO SAVE FOR THE FUTURE "Because you need to be prepared for whatever is coming your way. It's fine to say you don't want to retire as an excuse to get out of saving, but the future is unknown, and life happens—things and emergencies just pop up."

SAVING VS. PAYING OFF DEBT

Should you buy Google stock or pay off your student loans? Should you save money for your kid to go to college or pay off your car loan? Let's look at some real world dilemmas when it comes to choosing between saving or paying off debt, as well as strategies for how to tackle them.

YOU CAN'T DO EVERYTHING

Personal finance experts give all sorts of advice about what you should and shouldn't do. You should save for an emergency fund, but you should also pay off debt as quickly as possible. You should contribute to your 401(k), but you shouldn't spend more than you earn. But what do you do when you can't do everything?

You are going to have to weigh the pros and cons of each situation. How do you do this? There are a few rules that you can use as a guide.

It Depends on the Debt Most of us are told that debt is an evil thing. While it's far better to be debt-free than indebted, there are many cases where you can coexist with debt peacefully and productively. Mortgages and student loans are called good debt, since a student loan increases your income potential, while a house can be a great investment if it increases in value over time. In contrast, credit cards are generally bad debt since the interest rates are much higher. Somewhere between these two debt extremes are car loans, lines of credit, and other types of credit (see Table 28). The most important thing to keep in mind when evaluating your options is how much interest you're paying on your debt. That will help you determine if paying off your debt will save you more money in the long run.

It Depends on the Savings To decide whether you'll get more benefit from saving or from paying off debt, you need to understand the value of different savings vehicles. For example, you can rarely go wrong when choosing to contribute to a 401(k) with an employer match, rather than paying off debt. Since contributing to your 401(k) will allow you to get money from your employer that you wouldn't have otherwise gotten, you will be getting a much better return on your money. Investing in the stock market might also be a better plan than paying off a mortgage with a very low interest rate, since the average annual rate of return for investing in the stock market is often pegged around 7% to 8.5%. The challenge is that your return on investment varies with the investments you choose.

TABLE 28

GOOD DEBT VS. BAD DEBT

You want to pay down bad debt quickly because it often has high-interest rates, so you should prioritize that over savings. But good debt has lower interest rates, and you're often better off prioritizing savings over paying off good debt.

GOOD DEBT	BAD DEBT
Student loans	High-interest credit cards
Mortgages	Auto loans
Home equity line of credit	Borrowing from family
Low-interest loan or line of credit	Cash advance or payday loans

The most important thing to keep in mind when evaluating your savings options is how much you can expect to make in return, and if that return will exceed the amount you're paying in interest on the debts you have. Also, if you're having trouble, know that you're not alone (Figure 11).

It Depends on the Timing Interest rates and rates of return aren't static. If you got a great introductory offer of a low interest rate on a credit card for the first year, it might make sense to put some of your money into savings instead of paying off that debt, if you can be sure to pay it off before the interest rate increases.

MOST OF US ARE TOLD THAT DEBT IS AN EVIL THING

FIGURE 11

WHY AREN'T WE SAVING?

According to American Consumer Credit Counseling, consumers gave the following reasons for not being able to save:

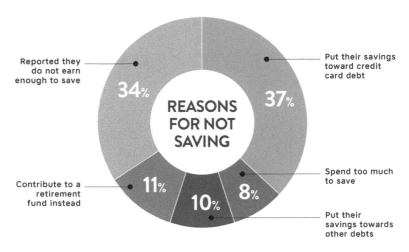

Reported they do not earn enough to save — 34%

Put their savings toward credit card debt — 37%

REASONS FOR NOT SAVING

Spend too much to save — 8%

Contribute to a retirement fund instead — 11%

Put their savings towards other debts — 10%

Source: ACCC[37]

WAYS TO USE MONEY, RANKED

Here is a quick cheat sheet to optimize how you deploy your money, based on which way will generally give you the best return on your dollar. Of course, not all financial experts agree that this is how you should prioritize using your money, and there are exceptions to the rules below. Make sure you evaluate all the variables and make the choice that is right for you.

1. **401(k) Match:** If your employer is matching your contributions, you will immediately get up to a 100% return on your investment. On top of that, you will be earning money on your investments and you'll get a tax break. This one is a no-brainer.

2. **High-Interest Credit:** After you contribute to your 401(k), the next thing you should tackle is any loans that have interest rates above 7.5%. Focus first on credit card debts as the interest rates on those are usually the highest.

HOW TO RESIST A SPLURGE
WHEN YOU GET A WINDFALL

Let's say you win $1,000 on the lottery, you get a $1,000 bonus, or the IRS sends you a $1,000 check. Getting money that you might not have expected can be exciting, especially if you've been cutting back and sacrificing your current wants for your long-term savings needs. If you have debt or you're behind on your savings plan, you should really be using this money more effectively. So what can you do to resist the urge to blow it all on a tablet or a new flat screen? The trick is to splurge just a little. Put 5% to 10% of your windfall aside to spend on yourself now. You might do something fun that will create a great memory, or you might buy something that will last a while like a piece of jewelry or sports equipment you'll use often. Every time you use that item, you'll remember your splurge and not feel like you're sacrificing everything.

3. **Emergency Fund:** If you ever have an emergency, it helps to have some cash on hand. Experts recommend saving enough to cover three to six months' worth of expenses. Some people recommend saving a small emergency fund before paying off debts.

4. **Health Savings Account:** If you have a health plan with a high deductible or if you have chronic health issues, an HSA is generally a good place to put your money. Since there are tax considerations for contributing to an HSA that are connected to your income, this will benefit some people more than others.

5. **Roth IRA:** Putting money in your IRA is a good plan for Millennials. Because you're still young, the money that you put into it will have a chance to grow significantly by the time you retire—and you won't have to pay interest on any of it.

6. **Save for a Down Payment:** If you don't own a home but plan to buy one in the next few years, saving for a down payment is important. Owning your own home is a crucial part of many people's retirement plans and can also be a great investment. If you do buy a home, it's important to try to pay a 20% down payment.

7. **College Savings:** While saving for your children's college costs in a 529 plan or a Coverdell account might seem like a pressing priority, you shouldn't put money into this pot until you're out of credit card debt and you're on track with saving for your retirement.

8. **Low-Interest Credit:** If you have loans with interest rates below 7.5%, then they will on average cost less to service than you will make by investing that money. Until you have maxed out other savings goals, don't worry about paying these loans off faster than you need to.

9. **Mortgage:** Some people want the psychological and financial freedom of being mortgage-free. Still, many personal finance experts and economists agree that when interest rates are low it makes more sense to invest your money for your future than pay down your mortgage. It's simple math: If you're paying 5% in interest on your mortgage and making 7.5% to 8% on your investments, then you're better off paying your mortgage off at the normal rate.

Student Loans Paying off your student loans and your mortgage are pretty much a tie if the interest rate you're paying on your mortgage and student loans are similar. If they aren't, then you should concentrate on paying down whichever has the highest rate.

LEARN TO LOVE YOUR DEBT

We often choose to pay down low-interest debt when we should really be saving and investing that money. How can we learn to love our debt? The first step is to recognize that it's normal. Debt is a part of life, and it helps us accomplish our goals. We shouldn't be fearful of it. The next step is to do a calculation to determine whether it will make sense to save or to pay down debt. Use a retirement calculator and a debt calculator so that you can see the numbers for yourself. Find a balance that will allow you to pay down debt at a rate that makes you feel comfortable while still saving money.

CHOOSING BETWEEN SAVING AND PAYING OFF DEBT

Saving and paying off debt are the first steps to getting rich, but what order should you be doing these in? I asked Nancy Gaines, who founded the blog *Women Gaining Wealth*, to talk about her experiences choosing between paying off debt and saving money.

ON HER OWN DECISIONS TO PAY OFF DEBT "There were several life events where you'll have to choose between savings and debt:

- **Decision to Pay Debt:** After graduate school, I decided to pay my student loans of almost $55,000 as fast as I could, so I would have money available to invest or buy real estate. Every bonus check, rebate check, raise, etc. went toward paying down debt. *Why:* My income after getting an MBA was almost double my pre-MBA earnings, so I felt confident that my salary could cover my living expenses while I paid off debt.

- **Decision to Pay Debt:** I left St. Louis to move to Denver and decided to make my house a rental home. There was about $50,000 left on the mortgage. Again, I poured every raise, bonus, tax refund, etc. into paying down the mortgage instead of saving. *Why:* I decided that I'd rather have rental income on a free and clear property so it was truly passive income."

ON WHAT FACTORS WOULD MAKE HER CHOOSE TO PAY OFF DEBT RATHER THAN SAVE "In both cases, I considered the following factors:

- Risk—what were the odds that I would need savings to cover some unexpected expense
- Tradeoffs—what was I giving up (interest, dividends, stock increases) for the peace of mind to reduce my debt
- Job Security—how worried was I about downsizing
- Alternative Uses of Money—was the return on another investment high enough not to pay off debt"

ON WHAT FACTORS MIGHT MAKE HER CHOOSE TO SAVE RATHER THAN PAY OFF DEBT "For saving, I considered the following factors:

- Timing of Upcoming Expenses—what did I need money for (major repairs, down payment on a house, down payment on a new car, annual life insurance premium payment, etc.)

- Tradeoffs—what was I giving up (interest, dividends, stock increases)

- Job Security—how worried was I about downsizing"

ON HOW TO FIND A BALANCE BETWEEN SAVING AND PAYING OFF DEBT "I would recommend your readers make a list of factors like I did in the above answers. Then score each factor to determine the best use of their money right now. Re-evaluate the criteria every 90 days while they determine if adjustments should be made. This gives people a chance to modify their decisions based on what's going on in their lives and the economy. It also takes the pressure of 'making the wrong decision' away so they don't get 'analysis paralysis.'"

ON HOW MILLENNIALS SHOULD PRIORITIZE HOW THEY USE THEIR MONEY "First, no matter what, save 10% for retirement! Find a way to live on 90% of your income. Second, save at least $2,000 in an emergency fund before paying down debt. Third, make sure your total debt is no more than 35% of your take-home pay. If it exceeds that amount, pay down debt to get it within that ratio. Finally, alternate savings with paying down debt every 3 months so you can focus on both goals."

15

INVESTING

By this point in your life, you've probably realized that you aren't going to be the lead singer in a famous rock band. You've also probably crunched the numbers and discovered that you're more likely to be elected president than to win the lottery. But don't give up on your dream of being a millionaire yet! In this chapter, we'll look at how to invest so that you can retire comfortably.

WAYS TO PUMP UP YOUR MONEY

Investing is like sending your money to the gym. Because of inflation, each year the money you have sitting in your checking and savings accounts is worth a little less. If your money sits around and eats Cheetos all day, it will get flabby and weak and it won't be able to do the things you need it to do in the future. The only way to pump your money up is to invest it (see Table 29).

Here are some common investments people make to keep their money growing enough to work for them, and do everything they need it to when retirement time comes.

Stocks Stocks are assets that are pretty easy to understand in principle. By owning stock, you own part of a company. Investing in stocks involves a certain degree of risk, because you can potentially lose money. Even among stocks, some are riskier than others. Still, so many investors choose to hold stocks as part of their portfolio because they have some of the highest growth potential compared to other types of investments (See Table 30 for key stock market vocabulary). In fact, according to Credit Suisse, the average long-term annualized return of stocks tends to be around 8.5%.[38]

TABLE 29
DON'T DELAY!

When I asked Lule Demmissie, managing director for TD Ameritrade, why Millennials shouldn't delay investing for their retirement, she told me the following: "Many Millennials think they should pay off their student loans first or that they don't make enough money to save for retirement right now. However, putting aside just $10, $25, or $100 each month can have a significant impact in long-term retirement savings."

$100 a month for 20 years starting at age 21 = $468,236
$100 a month for 20 years starting at age 41 = $95,039

In this scenario, the total cost of delaying retirement is $373,197!

TABLE 30

LIONS, TIGERS, AND BEAR MARKETS

TERM	DEFINITION
Bear Market	A bear market is when stock prices are falling or expected to fall.
Bull Market	A bull market is when stock prices are rising or expected to rise.
Volatility	Volatility refers to how much a particular stock is changing in price over a period of time. If there are significant price changes in a short period of time, the stock would be called volatile.
Yield	Yield refers to the return on an investment. This could refer to interest or dividends. It's usually referred to as a percentage of the investment's cost.
Initial Public Offering (IPO)	IPO is when the stock of a company is sold for the first time to the public.
Index	An index is a list of stocks that are grouped together to measure a portion or a whole of a market. For example the S&P 500 is an index that measures 500 of the strongest companies. You can't invest in an index, but you can invest in index funds.
Earnings Per Share (EPS)	This is the net income of the company divided by the amount of stock currently issued after they pay dividends to preferred stockholders.
P/E Ratio	This is the price-to-earnings ratio and measures the price per share divided by the annual earnings per share. Different industries have different P/E averages, and where a stock sits compared to that average can help you determine whether a stock is overpriced or underpriced.

Source: Investopedia.com

Mutual Funds A mutual fund is a pool of money from many different investors that is used to invest in a number of different types of investments. The investment strategy of a mutual fund is determined by a professional investor. If you don't have a lot of money to invest and want to have a diversified portfolio, a mutual fund is often a great way to achieve diversification.

When choosing a mutual fund, be careful to choose one with low-management fees. If your management fees are too high, it will eat into your investment returns, potentially costing you a significant amount over the long run.

Bonds A bond essentially involves loaning money to a corporate or government organization for a specific period of time at a specific rate of interest. You can purchase bonds from governments, states, municipalities, and companies. The bonds' interest rate is determined by the credit quality of the organization issuing the bond and the length of time of the loan. Bonds are considered to be fairly safe investments. Corporate bonds for companies facing potential bankruptcy present more risk, since you could have a problem getting your money back if the company goes under. If a company is facing financial risk and you still want to invest, buying a bond might be a better choice than buying a share since bonds get paid out in bankruptcy before shares.

Real Estate If you don't like all your assets invested in pieces of paper, you might consider investing in real estate. Buying a home to live in yourself is the most common form of real estate investing. Not only do you get to write off your mortgage interest on your tax return, but you can also potentially make money if the price of your home increases while you live in it. According to a study out of McGill University, for most Americans their principal residence accounts for 62% to 67% of their net worth.[39]

But there are ways to invest in real estate other than simply buying a principal residence. For example, you could buy a vacation property or a rental property. You could also buy a bigger home with a suite that you can rent.

If you do decide to dip your toe into property investments, make sure you figure out all the potential costs before buying anything.

WHY THE CASH MIGHT BE IN THE CONDO

When we think about investing, we usually think about buying stocks, bonds, or other pieces of virtual paper, but we should also consider investing in property according to Paula Pant of the great blog *Afford Anything*. She suggests if you want to go this route you should look at it as a source of cash flow. According to Paula, "There are two ways that investing is going to make you money. One way is by going up and down in value over time, and the other way is by paying out income. Houses are great sources of rental income. If you go into real estate, focus on getting that cash flow and think of appreciation purely as icing on the cake and a way to keep up with inflation."

High-Interest Savings Accounts High interest is a relative term in regards to savings accounts. In reality, a good high-interest account will pay around 1% to 3% in interest. While this is much better than a typical savings account or checking account, it is not nearly as good as many other investment options.

Unfortunately, for many people who haven't made a proper investment plan, their savings accounts play too big a role. Unless you're saving up for a down payment for a house or some other significant expense that you expect in the near future, you shouldn't have anything other than your emergency fund in your savings or checking accounts.

Exchange Traded Funds (ETF) ETFs are a hybrid of two different kinds of investment vehicles. ETFs are what you would get if a mutual fund and a stock mated and had a child. They are funds that often track various stock or bond indexes, but can also be managed funds. The difference is that they are traded on the stock market so their price is determined by demand like a stock. In a strictly legal sense, they are a corporation or a trust that owns assets and sells ownership in the form of shares to shareholders. Shareholders then share in the profits in the form of interest or dividends.

UNCOMMON INVESTMENT OPTIONS

Physical Gold You might have seen the infomercials about how the only safe way to invest in a volatile market is to buy gold. They usually play during newscasts or other programs that appeal to people over 60. Gold can be a good investment option, but if you're buying physical gold, you might have to find a way to store it and insure it. While it might not be as exciting as owning a big fat brick of gold, you can buy gold stocks or gold Exchange Trade Funds.

Options Options aren't for the casual investor. If you like investing and have been actively involved in managing your stock portfolio for a while, you might consider trading options.

There are two types of stock options: call options and strike options. Call options give you the right to purchase a stock at a particular price and strike options give you the right to sell a stock at a particular price. You buy call options when you think that the stock will increase in value and put strike options when you think it will decrease in value.

WE HAVE INVESTING PTSD

According to *Bankrate*, Millennials between the ages of 18 and 29 are three times more likely to have their net worth parked in savings accounts than hard at work in the stock market. While it's not surprising that a generation who came of age during a financial meltdown is risk-averse, it will hurt us in the long run. Money that's sitting in savings accounts won't keep pace with inflation and gradually will have less purchasing power. According to Bankrate, 39% of Millennials preferred to hold money they don't need for at least ten years in cash, 24% chose real estate, and 13% picked the stock market. If we have any hope of accomplishing our long-term goals, we need to change those numbers.

Futures Futures are similar to options in that you purchase a contract that gives you the right to buy something in the future at a particular price. The difference is that with futures you're purchasing a commodity instead of a stock—and you're obligated to buy it, rather than just having it as an option. While direct producers and direct consumers of commodities make up the backbone of the futures markets, many other people who have nothing to do with producing or directly consuming buy and sell futures in order to make money.

NOT ALL STOCKS ARE CREATED EQUAL

If you choose to stash your cash in the stock market, you should know that there are different kinds of stocks that you can choose from. Here are some of your options.

Dividend-Paying Stocks Dividend stocks pay a dividend—a one-time or routine payment to shareholders of the company's earnings. Companies that are more secure and more stable are more likely to pay dividends. Dividend stocks that pay regular dividends are known as income stocks, since they can provide the holder with a steady income. Many retirees or people approaching retirement invest in dividend stocks for this reason. Dividends are one way to accelerate the growth of your investments. You get a payment without having to sell the share.

Value Stocks Do you like looking for diamonds in the rough? If so, then value stocks might be right for you. Value stocks are stocks that are thought to be trading at a discount. Value investors look at the fundamentals of companies to see which ones have been unjustifiably put on the clearance table. If there is reason to believe that an undervaluation is temporary because, say, the business is still strong, it might be a good one to buy.

Small Cap These are stocks that have a relatively small market capitalization. While the definition of small cap varies depending on who you ask, according to Investopedia, these stocks are generally valued between $300 million and $2 billion. Because they are smaller and less established companies, they offer greater opportunities for growth but can be riskier.

Mid Cap These stocks make up the difference between small cap and large cap, generally referring to companies with market capitalizations of between $2 billion and $10 billion according to Investopedia. They tend to have some of the benefits from both large and small caps, being more stable like large caps and yet still often having an opportunity for further growth like small caps.

Large Cap Large-cap stocks refer to companies that are valued at more than $10 billion. These are big companies, many of which will be familiar to you. The focus in large cap stocks is on the market valuation. Twitter and Facebook would qualify as large cap stocks because they're valued at more than $10 billion.

Penny Stocks Penny stocks are stocks that trade for under $5, although most actually trade for only pennies. Penny stocks are the riskiest kinds of stocks, partly because the companies are either small or they have experienced financial difficulties and been delisted from the main exchanges. Many have very limited followings, meaning that few people buy and sell them, making it easy to manipulate or affect the price. Unless you know what you're doing, you're best advised to avoid this sector.

Blue Chip Stocks In many ways, blue chips are the cream of the crop of the stock market. They are large companies that are well-established and in good financial standing. They are companies that have been around for decades and are valued in the billions of dollars. Their names will often be familiar to you. Because of all these factors, blue chip stocks are often considered safe investments. The only downside is that because they're so big and stable, their growth is generally slower. If you're looking for a safe investment, these are the stocks to consider; if you're looking for big returns, you should look elsewhere.

Growth Stocks Growth stocks are stocks in companies that are expected to grow quickly in the coming years. Because they're focused on growth and reinvest profits into their business, they usually don't pay dividends. Technology companies and stocks from companies in emerging markets are often classified as growth stocks. Because these companies are expected to grow, their stock prices can often seem high compared to their current earnings. Because of that, any negative change in the expected future growth of the company can take a huge toll on the stock price.

Preferred Stocks Preferred stocks are a special kind of stock with special rights. Preferred shares might have different voting rights, and they often guarantee a fixed dividend. In addition, in the event of bankruptcy or liquidation, preferred shareholders will be paid before common shareholders. A company can choose to have some of their stock as common stock and another portion of their stocks as preferred stocks. Many investors find preferred stocks attractive because of their guaranteed dividends.

HAVE MORE THAN ONE BASKET

Diversifying your investment portfolio is like applying for more than one college. In the mix, you will have some investments such as bonds, which you can count on like safety schools. You will also have some investments with the potential for a higher return but less certainty, like stocks and mutual funds—your dream or stretch schools. A diversified portfolio includes the following:

Diverse Assets Historically, different kinds of assets perform better under different market conditions. By spreading your portfolio across various categories, you ensure that you will more consistently be able to see gains. If you are invested too heavily in the wrong kinds of assets, you can end up with less money for your retirement.

Diverse Industries A diverse portfolio includes not just different kinds of assets but also exposure to different industries. For example, if all of your stocks and mutual funds are invested in social media stocks like Facebook, Twitter, and LinkedIn, and something goes wrong, you could potentially see a good portion of your portfolio's value disappear overnight. You need to ensure that your money is spread across different industries so that if one industry does badly it won't ruin your entire investment future. See Table 31 for some popular investment strategies.

TABLE 31

POPULAR INVESTMENT STRATEGIES

STRATEGIES	HOW TO DO IT
Buy and Hold	Choose investments that you think will perform well over the long term and hold onto them for a long time.
Dollar-Cost Averaging	Buy shares in the same investments over a period of time rather than all at once. This reduces the risk of putting all your money in before a downturn.
Income Investing	Choose investments that provide regular income in the form of dividends or other payouts.
Momentum Investing	Choose investments that have had high returns over the last 3 to 12 months and sell those that have had poor returns over the same period.
Day Trading	Day trading is not for new traders and is generally quite risky. Day traders trade based on anticipated short-term changes in stock prices and buy and sell over short periods of time.
Value Investing	Select stocks that are priced low relative to their value. Value investors look for stocks that have a low P/E ratio for their industry or have been sold off because of bad news that doesn't affect the company's long-term prospects.
Growth Investing	Seek out stocks whose earnings are expected to grow faster than the market average. Growth stocks often have high P/E ratios because the growth is priced into their prices, and if they don't meet expectations, it can lead to quick drops in their stock price.
Index Investing	Buy index funds for different indexes. These funds provide you with low cost investments that give you a diverse portfolio.

Source: Investopedia.com

100K BY 30: WHY STARTING EARLY IS IMPORTANT

Here is a story about saving for retirement that may shock you. It starts with two brothers. One brother is a saver who started putting money aside in his early twenties to invest for his retirement. By the time he was 30, he had $100,000 invested in the stock market. The other brother who was five years older had other priorities and didn't start investing for retirement until he was 35. The younger brother didn't put any more money into his investment account after he turned 30, whereas the older brother diligently put $10,000 a year into his account for the next 35 years, investing a total of $350,000. Can you guess who would have more money when they retired at 65, assuming an average 7% annual return on their investments? The brother who stopped investing when he turned 30 would have $1,150,615.18, while the brother who had started investing at 35 would have $1,065,601.21. This is the magic of compound interest. If you can manage to save $100,000 by the time you turn 30, you will have $1 million when you turn 65 without saving any more money.

WHY SHOULD I INVEST?

To help with advice on investments, I sat down with Robert Farrington, who is the founder of the website *The College Investor* and known by many as America's Millennial Money Expert.

WHEN DID HE START INVESTING? "I stared investing when I was in high school. I got my first job at 16 and started saving, then took $500 and started investing. Honestly, I started investing because I saw and read about people like Warren Buffett who made billions doing it."

WHAT HAS HE BEEN ABLE TO ACCOMPLISH BY INVESTING? "Investing has allowed me to build a lifestyle that I want. By starting early, in my teens, I was able to save and grow it through investing to give me enough money for a down payment on a house. Furthermore, investing has allowed me the comfort in knowing that I can retire anytime without relying on government programs like Social Security. Every year I add to my investments through my earnings and at the same time watch them grow."

WHAT THREE PIECES OF ADVICE DOES HE HAVE FOR MILLENNIALS STARTING TO INVEST? "If you are considering getting started investing, I would say you need to do the following:

1. Have an emergency fund separate from your investments. You need to keep cash on hand for emergencies, that isn't invested in the stock market.

2. Have goals for investing and understand your risk tolerance and timeframe. For example, if your goal is saving for retirement, you set up a timeframe of 40 years. Then, know that the market will go up and down, but you still have your timeframe.

3. Remember that investing is designed for the long term, which is more than 20 years."

HIS THREE FAVORITE INVESTING TIPS "My top investing tips are really, really simple. For 99% of investors, you should:

1. Stick to low-cost index funds that match the market return.

2. Take these index funds and build a diversified portfolio that matches an allocation you're comfortable with. Then rebalance one to two times per year.

3. Continue to invest regularly. Whether it's in an IRA or 401(k), just keep investing.

With these three tips combined, you'll amass a very large portfolio by the time you retire."

WHY MILLENNIALS SHOULD PAY MORE ATTENTION TO THEIR INVESTMENT PLANS "Millennials have an advantage over other investors—time. The power of compounding will help Millennials by magnitudes if they get started earlier.

Second, many Millennials are leaving free money on the table. If you have a job that offers a 401(k) match, you need to be taking advantage of it."

SOME OF THE BEST INVESTMENTS HE'S MADE "I love Warren Buffett's advice: 'Be fearful when others are greedy and greedy when others are fearful.' That advice led me to investing a lot of money in the fall of 2008 when the markets were near all-time lows. Since then, those investments have doubled in value."

HACKS

TAXES AND INVESTING

Maximizing your tax savings when you invest is important if you want to make sure that you have more money when you retire. Tax-sheltered accounts like 401(k)s and IRAs are great ways to grow your investments, while either avoiding tax or deferring it. Another investment strategy that helps you save on taxes is investing in US companies that pay dividends. Taxpayers get a break on dividends since they are only taxed at 15%. Similarly, you get a tax break on capital gains on stocks that you've held for more than one year; they are taxed at 15% for everyone but the highest income earners. Remember that you can also offset any capital gains you have in a year through your capital losses.

USE THE 1% RULE

When buying real estate as an investment, Paula Pant from *Afford Anything* suggests you look for properties that meet the 1% rule. According to Paula, "That means that the rent should be 1% of the total acquisition cost." By the total acquisitions cost, Paula means the purchasing price, closing costs, and cost of any repairs needed. She gives the following example: "Let's say that you buy the house for $90,000, and it has $2,000 worth of closing costs and it needs $8,000 worth of repairs. You have $100,000 invested in it, and that means it needs to rent for at least $1,000 a month. If it doesn't meet that minimum criterion, then you should skip it and look for something else."

HAVE A THREE-FUND PORTFOLIO

Keeping your investment strategy simple is often the key to ensuring you actually take action. According to Paula, you should consider buying just three funds to make up your portfolio. She chooses three specific types of fund: "One of which would be a total US stock market index fund, one of which is a total international market index fund, and one of which is the total bond market index fund. The reason why a three-fund portfolio is so helpful for a new investor is that if you look at too many options, you might just go into what's called analysis paralysis, where you're so overwhelmed by all of that information that you don't act and you let your money sit in a savings account, which is the worst thing you could do."

BE YOUR OWN REAL ESTATE AGENT

Your home is an investment, so why give a significant portion of that investment to a real estate agent? If your house is in an area where houses are selling well, you might get away with listing it yourself. If you intend to do so, make sure you get it professionally appraised before you set your price. A professional appraiser will help you determine what you can get for your home based on its features and how much other similar homes are currently selling for. Then you need to create a one-page listing feature of your home with pictures, get your property listed wherever possible, and put up a for-sale sign. You should stage your home to make sure it looks nice and practice showing your home to potential buyers. Finally, get a lawyer to handle the sales contract for you to make sure that everything is done properly.

401(K) HACKS

Contributing to your 401(k) should be a priority, especially if your employer is offering you a matching contribution. If meeting their match seems impossible, consider breaking it down to a monthly or weekly contribution to get your head around it. Pay more attention to your 401(k) to make sure that the money that is in there is working properly for you. Ensure that you have the right asset allocation, and that you're not paying too much in fees. Review your 401(k) every year and make changes as needed.

ROTH IRA HACKS

A Roth IRA is a great thing for Millennials. You put post-tax money into it, and it grows over the years; then, when you retire and it's worth much more than you put into the account, you will pay no tax on what you take out. Even if you have a 401(k), you should consider opening a Roth IRA as well. A Roth IRA is also a sneaky way to potentially save money to help your kids go to college. According to Libby Kane from LearnVest, money saved in your Roth IRA isn't counted when schools calculate financial aid, whereas money saved in a 529-plan is. That means that you'll be offered more financial aid from the schools and you'll be able to exceed your annual 529-plan contribution limits by using an IRA as well. While there are some fees when withdrawing money early from a Roth IRA, you can get around them by withdrawing only the principal and not the interest.

DON'T PANIC

You've worked hard for your money. When the stock market starts to shift in a downward direction, you might be tempted to pull back and sell everything. If you do, you might find yourself regretting it later. Stock markets fluctuate; if you sell at the wrong point, you're likely to lock in your losses and not be able to take advantage of the upside when the stock market recovers. Rather than trying to time the market, make investments for the long term. Over time, you'll be rewarded.

BE CAREFUL IF YOU RATE-CHASE

Rate-chasing for credit cards or for savings accounts can be time-consuming; it can also lead to pitfalls you hadn't anticipated. For example, you might find a card that offers you 0% interest for transferring money, but it might only be for six months. If you can't pay off your balance in that time, make sure you have a plan for what to do when the higher interest rate inevitably kicks in. Similarly, many people shop around for better interest rates on savings accounts. Sometimes banks offer higher rates for the first few months and then switch you back to an interest rate that's much lower. Make sure you read all the fine print to ensure that you're getting the best deal.

CLIMB THE PROPERTY LADDER

Depending on how stable your local real estate market is, many young couples find that buying a small property and developing equity is a necessary step to buying their dream homes. If you plan on staying in your smaller place long enough for the property to appreciate to a point where you will make money selling it, you will then have equity to put toward your next real estate purchase. This equity allows you to afford buying a bigger and more expensive home because you will need a smaller mortgage to do so. Some people buy and sell real estate and slowly move up the property ladder until they can afford to buy their dream homes. If you plan on doing this, just be careful; you can also lose money if property values go down.

AUTOMATE YOUR INVESTING

Why do things consciously when you can set up a process and never have to worry about it again? Robert Farrington from *The College Investor* suggests that you make investing easier by taking the hard work out of it. He says, "Automate, automate, automate. Millennials want things done for them—and it can be done with investing as well. Set up a 401(k) plan to invest automatically. Set up a brokerage account to auto-debit your checking account and invest automatically. You can set up your investment life to be auto-mated just like every other aspect of your life."

OPT FOR A DIVIDEND-REINVESTMENT PLAN

If you own stocks that pay dividends, consider signing up for a dividend reinvestment plan (DRIP). With a DRIP, the money that you would have received as a dividend is automatically reinvested in the stock that paid you the dividend. This allows you to gradually build the number of shares you own—and, in turn, your dividend income. There are many benefits to reinvesting your dividends. First, by doing so via a DRIP, you do not have to pay brokerage fees for the transaction. Another benefit is the fact that it is automated, which means that you don't have to remember each time a dividend is paid out to reinvest the money. If you believe that the price of a stock you own will continue to go up, then DRIPs are a great way to invest. Most online brokerages will offer DRIPs, and that is the easiest way to set one up. There is also a way to set one up directly through the company whose stock you own, but that can be more complex. The benefit, however, of doing it that way is that you'll be able to buy fractions of stocks.

KEEP YOUR COSTS LOW

Costs like brokerage fees and mutual fund fees add up. A 2% mutual fund fee might not seem like a lot, but it can mean tens or hundreds of thousands of dollars less when you retire because of the compound interest you will lose out on over the years. It's the same with brokerage fees: $10 to $30 seems cheap until you start adding them up. To cut down on fees, choose a low-fee mutual fund or a no-fee index fund or ETF. Find an online brokerage that offers low fees and make fewer transactions. Choose stocks that you're very confident will do well over the long term and buy a significant amount of each stock; then, hold it for a long period of time rather than trading your stocks frequently.

FIND THE BEST ONLINE BROKER

When you're investing your own money in stocks online, make sure you're getting the best deal in regard to online brokerage accounts, since the fees can eat into your returns and cost you thousands over the long haul. If you think $7 trades sound good, then consider the cheap trades you can get at sites like TradeKing, Trade Monster, and Options-House. TradeKing charges $4.95, Trade Monster charges $4.95, and OptionsHouse charges $4.75. Shop around to find a site that is best for you at a price that you're willing to pay.

SHOULD YOU BUY A FIXER-UPPER?

Buying a home that needs a bit of work can be a great investment, or it can lead to your financial ruin. Be aware that even small renovations can be a lot of work. Contractors are notoriously unreliable when they're working on small jobs. I know people who have had their kitchens torn up for weeks longer than they were initially promised because their contractors kept taking bigger jobs before finishing the work on their homes. Before you buy, make sure you know what needs to be done and how much it will cost. Be sure to add a 25% buffer into the estimated costs so that you're not caught off guard in case things cost more than the price you're quoted. Also, make sure that the renovations you intend to make will actually add value to the house and that you're not just sinking money into renovations that won't pay off later. Don't buy a house with any structural issues or in need of any other types of repairs that will cost a lot of money.

OPEN A NO-FEE CHECKING ACCOUNT

One of the most unnecessary expenses is bank fees. You are literally paying for access to your money. When you deposit your money at a bank, they are getting to use your money to lend out to other people. That means that they're making money off of you. If your bank is also trying to charge you to access your own money, it's time to send your bank packing and find a bank that treats its customers better.

OPEN A HIGH-INTEREST SAVINGS ACCOUNT

I know too many people who let their savings languish in low-interest checking or savings accounts. It's the equivalent of throwing money away. You need to maximize how your money works for you by putting short-term savings like emergency funds or down payments for a home in high-interest savings accounts. These accounts will earn 1% to 3% more than most other bank accounts. This will mean $10 to $30 more in interest per year for every $1,000 you have in there. If you have $10,000 in that account, that's $100 to $300 more a year for doing nothing other than moving your money.

OPTIMIZE YOUR BANK ACCOUNTS

You might stand in line to get a good deal on a new TV, but when was the last time you went shopping for a good deal on your bank accounts? Check in periodically to see if you're getting the best value. Is there a bank that would offer you a better interest rate on your savings account or lower fees on your checking account? Is there one that is offering a promotion where you can get something free or a lower rate? Find the right accounts for your needs and you'll save.

DEPOSIT YOUR CHECKS WITH YOUR PHONE

Many banks are allowing you to take a picture of your check and deposit it that way. You don't need to go into the branch or even find an ATM; you just need to take out your smartphone. This might save you a bus fare or some money in gas, but that's not the point. It will save you time, and your time is valuable.

CONSIDER A CREDIT UNION

When you opt for a credit union instead of a big bank, you'll get great benefits and savings. For example, credit unions often offer lower account fees, better rates for borrowing, and higher interest rates for saving. They also often offer better customer service and pay you a share of their profits. What I love most about my local credit union is that they donate a significant chunk of their profits to my local community.

STAGGER YOUR BUYING

If you have a significant amount of money that you'd like to invest in bonds, stocks, or mutual funds, it can often be beneficial for you to stagger your buying over a period of several months. Since the stock market goes up and down over time, this will protect you from the risk of investing the full amount right before a downturn.

LOOK AT INSIDER BUYING

If you were the president of the company and thought that your company was doing terribly, would you buy that company's stock? Probably not. Neither would most corporate officers at publicly traded companies. In fact, when insiders buy their own stock, this is often seen as a good indication that they expect their company to do well in the future. Insider buying can be a good indicator of the potential for strong long-term returns.

ONLY INVEST WHAT YOU CAN LOSE

If you need to pay your taxes at the end of the year and you have money put aside for that purpose, should you invest it in the interim? That depends on how likely you think the IRS will be willing to accept the explanation that you lost your tax dollars in the stock market.

If you're hoping to buy a house in the near future and need money for your down payment or if you have money set aside that you think you might need to pay your bills, you should not invest that money. Only invest money that you can potentially afford to lose. While your likelihood of losing that money depends on how risky an investment you're purchasing, even the safest investments involve a degree of risk.

OVERCOME THE SUNK-COST FALLACY

If you put money in the stock market or another type of investment and you lose part of your initial investment, research shows that you are more likely to stick with that stock because of the hope or the belief that the stock will rebound and make back you money. The reason is that you have chosen that investment and are emotionally invested in that choice. You also believe subconsciously that by selling that investment your loss will then be real. Most of the time you would be better off selling that losing investment and investing your money in something that has a better likelihood of giving you a return. The challenge is that you are often not operating rationally. When we make a choice that doesn't pan out, we are often much more committed to it than if it did. By recognizing that you might have a tendency to behave in this way and instead rationally reevaluating all of your investments, you're more likely to make decisions that will be better for you in the long run.

RENT YOUR PROPERTIES

If you've invested in real estate for the purpose of rental income, one of the worst things you'll face is vacancies. For every month that there are no tenants in your rental property, you have to pay for the mortgage and expenses yourself. That loss can be devastating to your budget even if it's just a short-term issue. Luckily, there are things you can do to increase the likelihood of your rental property being leased and to ensure that good tenants stay for longer. The first thing you need to do is ensure that when you buy your rental property, it is in a location where people want to rent. If there are a lot of vacancies in that area, this is an indication that there probably isn't a lot of demand. When you do advertise your unit, be sure to take pictures that stage it in the best possible light. Tidy up rooms and arrange the furniture so that it looks more spacious. Make sure to take photos during the day in order to show off the natural light.

Advertise through the proper channels. Do your research to determine which websites are most used in your area for searching for housing. You might also consider making some small improvements, such as painting or updating flooring, that will have a big impact. When you do have good tenants, make sure to treat them well and respond to any of their concerns quickly. You might even consider giving them bonuses or breaks on the rent if they sign on to rent for another year.

BUY ON FEAR

Downturns in the market are often exacerbated because investors get scared and sell their investments. Because of this, the market often dips even further. When other investors are fearful, instead of drinking the Kool-Aid and selling off your holdings, consider it an excellent time to buy stocks that you see as having the potential for strong long-term returns. By buying when people are fearful, you're more likely to get a better price and greater returns. While almost no one can call the bottom, by buying during downturns you increase the potential upside of your investment, even if it continues to go down after you buy.

SET UP A STOP-LOSS

Sometimes life happens. You get busy, you don't check your investments, and the next thing you know you've lost 20% to 30% of your equity in one or more stocks. If you know you can't check your stocks every day, consider setting up a stop-loss measure on your investments. Stop-losses allow you to limit your loss should a stock decrease in value. What you do is you put a sell order in, specifying to sell your stock if it dips 10%, 15%, 20%, or 30% below its value. This ensures that you don't lose more than you can afford to lose.

START WITH FAMILIAR STOCKS

People often tell you to buy what you know when you're first starting to invest. The reason why this is so often suggested is that it makes it easier for you to learn about investing. You already know that McDonalds makes delicious fries, so you're certain that it will make delicious profits for you as well. By buying into companies you're already familiar with, you don't have to work so hard to understand their business models. This will make it easier to start investing and give you some momentum to keep learning about the stock market. The problem with buying familiar stocks is that most likely these companies are going to be selling consumer goods. If you only buy stocks that you know, then your portfolio isn't going to be properly diversified. So, start with what you know, but branch out into other areas.

BE WARY OF NEW THINGS: BITCOIN

Bitcoin has been hailed by the tech world as the next big thing, and it's skyrocketed in price from when it was first launched, but should you be investing your hard-earned money into Bitcoin or any other crypto-currency? One of the main downsides of putting all your money into Bitcoin is that there is nothing you can do if it's stolen. If you have cash in your bank account and it's hacked and stolen, your bank will give you that money back, but if your Bitcoin wallet is hacked, your money is gone for good. Another downside of investing in Bitcoin is that the market is very volatile, swinging up or down based on new regulations governing Bitcoins or merchants either deciding to accept or to stop accepting Bitcoin. While it might seem attractive to make some money on that potential volatility, it's a highly risky investment; don't put any money into it that you can't afford to lose.

TAKE YOUR DEDUCTIONS

A lot of people know that you can deduct your retirement contributions to you IRA or 401(k), but not everyone remembers to do so come tax time. Don't forget to take all the deductions that you can. For example, you can deduct 20% to 35% of the cost of daycare and summer camp with the Child and Dependent Care Credit. Also, you can deduct your medical expenses if they total more than 10% of your gross income, and if you move for work, you can also deduct your moving expenses.

AFTERWORD

COMPOUND INTEREST IS YOUTH'S
"FREE GIFT WITH PURCHASE"

If you're like us, you cringe when you see articles with the word "Millennials" in the title. If the writer isn't saying that we're lazy or unable to function in the workplace, they're saying that we're financially doomed because of something that we're supposedly doing wrong.

The people writing these articles are often from different generations. Maybe in their time they were able to make enough money from a summer job to pay their tuition. They got hired relatively easily after graduating and had a decent starting salary. They spent their lives working for the same company. They enjoy pensions and benefits that were cut before we even entered the workforce. When they'll retire, they are confident that Social Security and Medicare will take care of them.

In contrast, we came of age in an era where we needed a Bachelor's degree or even a Master's degree just to get a decent job. We paid much more in tuition than any other generation and racked up much more student-loan debt.[40] We entered the workforce during one of the biggest recessions and longest recoveries since the Great Depression. We struggled to get jobs, and those that did were often underemployed.[41] Our employers gave us lower starting salaries[42] in our first jobs and were less loyal to us than to the generations who preceded us, hiring many of us on contract or as freelancers. We will work at many companies over the course of our careers. Most of us won't have pensions, and many of us aren't covered by company benefits. When we retire, we're not sure if Social Security and Medicare will even be around anymore.

We are a generation that came of age during a meltdown on Wall Street. We watched many of our parents, friends, and relatives lose their homes, their cars, their jobs, or a large portion of their net worth. As a result, we're cautious and conservative. We are more likely than previous generations to hold our money in cash instead of investing. We're less likely than any other generation to have credit cards. We've got a long road to climb to financial freedom, but we're hopeful that things will get better and we'll be able to do it.

Our financial goals are different from those of the generations that came before us as well. We want more flexibility in our work lives, and we're willing to make less money to achieve that. We're more likely than other generations to start or want to start a business or startup.[43] We value travel, experiences, and education. We don't all want to own cars, since many of us prefer to bike or use car-sharing services. We want to make a difference through our work, and crave to feel valued. We want to pay off our student loans some day. We plan to buy a house in the city instead of the suburbs. Most of us want to have children, but we want to do it on our own terms. We are a generation fueled by disruptive technologies and new paradigms. Our lives will not look like the lives of anyone who came before us.

We're the most educated generation in history, but not all of us are doing well with our finances; we need help, but not a lecture in scaremongering. We are an amazing generation made up of millions who are collectively and individually making a difference and transforming the world. It's time that people stopped criticizing us and started helping us be successful on our own terms.

We don't have time to write down everything we spend, but we'll use an app to track it for us. We don't want to go to an old guy to learn about financial planning; we would rather Skype with a Millennial planner who understands our goals better. We want our budgets to be automated and our investment plans to be online.

Millennials are the first American generation that isn't expected to do as well as their parents. Experts predict that the Millennial middle class will struggle and that the divide between the 1% and the 99% will get bigger.[44] We are facing slumping wages and setbacks from years of being unemployed or underemployed. It seems like the world is trying to snatch our dreams from us. You might even say that we are in a fight for our future.

When it comes to preparing for that future, money *is* everything. Money is the ability to travel the world. It's time with loved ones and experiences that we will never forget. It's the ability to work for a nonprofit instead of a multinational. It's the certainty of knowing that we will be okay when we leave a job we hate, or have kids, or retire someday. It's the hope that we will someday pay off our student loans or own a house or go back to college. Money is the underwriter to all of our dreams. It is one of the most important parts of our lives because of how profoundly it affects all other aspects.

The most important message to close this book with is that, as Millennials, we have one great advantage over all the other generations that are older than us: we are still young. While the boomers and Generation X struggle to get their act together before they retire, we still have the time, the energy, and the capacity to do so with much less struggle. For every $1,000 we put away for our retirement now, Generation X will have to save around $2,000, and boomers will have to save around $4,000. Compound interest is like youth's "free gift with purchase." Take advantage of it.

We can make up for all the bad hands we've been dealt as a generation by getting serious about digging ourselves out of debt and starting to save for the future, but we have to start *now*. If your life was like a *Choose Your Own Adventure* novel, this would be one of the moments when the story branches off in two directions. You can choose to keep making all the financial mistakes you're making now, and you won't be able to meet your financial goals in the future. Or, you choose to change your life and save for the future. Now is the time to make your choice.

If you choose to change your life, then use this book as your roadmap. Take the first step toward a better financial future today. Do one thing. Then do another. You're not too busy to create a financial plan. Your life and your dreams are too important.

Once you get started, remember not to give up. Financial planning is a long-term process, and sometimes it can feel like you're not getting anywhere. But if you keep taking one step after another, you will eventually arrive at your destination.

ENDNOTES

1   www.youtern.com/thesavvyintern/index.php/2013/10/09/25-jobs-in-the
    -next-50-years-is-gen-y-really-ready/

2   www.bizjournals.com/albuquerque/news/2012/08/30/study-finds-that
    -millennials-change.html

3   www.worldatwork.org/adimLink?id=73898

4   www.advisorperspectives.com/dshort/updates/Household-Incomes-by
    -Age-Brackets.php

5   www.northwesternmutual.com/news-room/financial-planning-obstacles.aspx

6   www.consumerreports.org/cro/2013/08/best-time-to-buy-things/index.htm

7   healthymeals.nal.usda.gov/features-month/whats-season

8   www.bcgperspectives.com/content/articles/consumer_insight_marketing
    _millennial_consumer/

9   www.theatlantic.com/business/archive/2012/03/why-dont-young-americans
    -buy-cars/255001/

10 http://www.pewsocialtrends.org/2010/02/24/millennials-confident
    -connected-open-to-change/

11 www.autotrader.com/research/article/car-shopping/167808/4-questions
    -to-help-you-decide-on-a-new-or-used-car.jsp

12 consumerreports.org/cro/2013/04/best-worst-used-cars/index.htm

13 www.pewsocialtrends.org/files/2010/10/Millennials-confident-connected
    -open-to-change.pdf

14 www.theatlantic.com/business/archive/2014/11/why-its-so-hard-for
    -millennials-to-figure-out-where-to-live/382929

15 www.zillow.com/mortgage-rates/buying-a-home/pre-approval/

16 http://www.consumerfinance.gov/askcfpb/1791/what-debt-income-ratio
    -why-43-debt-income-ratio-important.html

17 www.bankrate.com/finance/mortgages/risks-of-walking-away-from
    -mortgage-debt-1.aspx

18 time.com/money/3178364/millennials-insurance-why-resist-coverage

19 www.resolve.org/family-building-options/making-treatment-affordable
    /the-costs-of-infertility-treatment.html

20 www.cheapair.com/blog/travel-tips/when-should-you-buy-your-airline
    -ticket-heres-what-our-data-has-to-say

21 www.cheapair.com/blog/travel-tips/when-to-ignore-our-advice-and-book
    -your-flight-as-early-as-possible/

22 www.farecompare.com/travel-advice/when-to-buy/

23 marketbusinessnews.com/credit-score-people-dont-know/3889

24 www.experian.com/credit-education/what-is-a-good-credit-score.html

25 creditcards.lovetoknow.com/What_is_a_Good_Credit_Score

26 www.myfico.com/crediteducation/whatsinyourscore.aspx

27 myFICO.com

28 www.consumerfinance.gov/askcfpb/318/how-do-i-get-and-keep-a-good
    -credit-score.html

29 www.wikihow.com/Prevent-Identity-Theft

30 www.wikihow.com/Prevent-Identity-Theft

31 blogs.wsj.com/numbers/congratulations-to-class-of-2014-the-most
    -indebted-ever-1368/

32 www.theatlantic.com/business/archive/2014/01/highly-educated-highly-
    indebted-the-lives-of-todays-27-year-olds-in-charts/283263

33 myFICO.com

34 www.moneytalksnews.com/ask-stacy-how-can-i-destroy-high-interest-debt/

35 www.consumerreports.org/cro/magazine-archive/november-2009/money
    /credit-cards/overview/credit-cards-ov.htm

36 www.credit.com/debt/understanding-your-debt-collection-rights/

37 www.consumercredit.com/financial-education/infographics/infographic
    -more-than-8-in-10-americans-prioritize-paying-down-debt-rather-than
    -saving-for-the-future.aspx

38 www.moneysense.ca/columns/what-are-normal-stock-market-returns

39 http://budgeting.thenest.com/percentage-net-worth-should-homes-value
    -be-33179.html

40 www.theguardian.com/money/us-money-blog/2013/dec/06/student-loan
    -debt-minimum-poverty-wage-jobs

41 www.cnbc.com/id/101427859

42 www.forbes.com/sites/meghancasserly/2011/01/05/the-new-pay-gap
    -boomers-millennials-salary-recession-raise/

43 www.kauffman.org/newsroom/2012/11/an-entrepreneurial-generation
    -of-18-to-34yearolds-wants-to-start-companies-when-economy-rebounds
    -according-to-new-poll

44 www.salon.com/2013/09/13/10_reasons_millennials_are_screwed_partner

INDEX

Boldface type is used to indicate apps.